MODEL ANSWERS

MODEL ESSAYS

by

J. R. Watson

Edited by D. C. Perkins

CELTIC REVISION AIDS

CELTIC REVISION AIDS
Lincoln Way, Windmill Road,
Sunbury on Thames, Middlesex

First published in this edition 1979

ISBN 017 751108 7

Printed in Hong Kong

CONTENTS

Page

1. Try to piece together your recollections of the days before you started school. 1
2. The countryside in winter. 3
3. A seaside resort at night. 4
4. Your school is organising a function to which parents and friends are invited. Its purpose is to raise money for some new equipment, amenity or venture. Write a circular letter to parents and friends describing the function and explaining the project. 6
5. Write a story entitled 'Never Again'. 8
6. Describe a country which you have been to or which you have read about. 10
7. A famous traitor in history or fiction. 12
8. Write a letter to the editor of your local newspaper, setting out your views on a proposal to ban smoking in places of entertainment. 15
9. Describe your thoughts during a walk at night. 17
10. A violent storm or blizzard has occurred in the area where you live. Compose a report for a local newspaper about its effects on transport and communications. 18
11. Describe the scene in an examination room 20
12. Maps and map makers. 22
13. Discuss a book that you have read. 24
14. Travel in an earlier century. 28
15. Describe the buildings you would see driving through your home town. 31
16. Give an account of the life of a famous scientist. 33
17. Tell the story of how you came upon a scene of desolation. 36

Page

18. Give an account of the life of a man or woman whom you admire. 39
19. A famous Cathedral. 42
20. Which country would you like to visit? Give reasons for your choice. 45
21. Write an article suitable for a magazine describing the attractions for the holidaymaker of one of the following–a small seaside town, a small village , a small holiday camp. 47
22. Write a character sketch of your doctor or dentist. 48
23. Explain to a foreigner the main duties of the English police force. 50
24. Describe a local character whom you find interesting. 52
25. What are the problems of transport in your home district. 54
26. A famous inventor. 56
27. Write about any film you have seen which impressed you. 60
28. Describe a scene you will never forget. 63
29. Describe a character whom you disliked and can never forget. 65
30. Describe a thunderstorm. 67
31. Write an essay on an important scientific discovery. 68
32. Write a review of a book you enjoyed reading. 70
33. 'The cinema is doomed because it cannot compete with television'—comment. 73
34. Write an essay about an inventor whom you would like to have known. 76
35. Is space research and travel a waste of time and money, or will it one day be of value to mankind. 80
36. A famous explorer. 82

Page

37. Describe the uniform or clothing worn and equipment used by one of the following— a hockey goal keeper, a nurse, a mountaineer, a wicket keeper. 85

38. 'Some see the motor car as a miraculous invention: others see it as man's greatest misfortune yet'. Discuss. 86

39. Give an account of a great engineering feat that you have seen or read about. 89

40. Describe a small town or village which has interested you. 92

41. Tell a story, showing how you had an accident because you failed to take care. 94

42. Write a story entitled 'My First Car'. 96

43. Going to church. 98

44. What are the threats to the future of wildlife? How can these threats be avoided? 101

PREFACE

This book of model essays is designed for all students who have to sit formal written examinations in the English language. The essays will be found most useful by those studying English for their 'O' and 'A' levels, R.S.A. and the Chamber of Commerce examinations. Professional students needing English for preliminary and intermediate certificates will find the argumentative and discussion type topics very helpful. The 'pegs' provided in the essay plans are good starting points for their own work.

Anyone using this book is advised to consult 'Aids to Essay Writing' by D. C. Perkins, which explains the various ways in which different types of essays may be tackled.

The prepared essays which follow, like others in the series, are not intended to be learned parrot-fashion and to be produced verbatim in examintation papers. They are intended as a guide to examination preparation and technique and if used properly will help you to produce your own carefully planned essays under examintaion conditions. The suggested time needed for each essay is given in brackets after the title.

INTRODUCTION

English essays, devised for public examinations, fall into the following main categories: descriptive, explanatory, argumentative, discursive and narrative. Many are a combination of these and examiners expect good candidates to be able to, for example, describe and argue, or explain and tell a story in a sustained piece of continuous prose.

The aim of this book of model essays is to help students by suggesting ideas and outlining ways of presenting them. There is no magical formula for good writing and the whole process involves much hard work.

There are five main factors that examiners take into consideration when grading student essays. These are (i) mechanical accuracy; (ii) vocabulary; (iii) syntax; (iv) content; (v) arrangement of material. To do really well at this paper, the work is expected to be free from mechanical errors and the candidate must show a thorough mastery of sentence construction. These sentences must not only be correct but also varied in length, pattern and rhythm. Good essayists have a wide vocabulary and choose words sensitively and judiciously. The essay must be well arranged with a clearly defined introduction, middle and rounding-off conclusion. Arguments should be presented cogently; essential details must stand out clearly in description and there should be variety of pace and emphasis in narrative work. Superior essays show originality and a good grasp of the topic; the material is logically presented with adequate linkage between paragraphs. Information used may come from the writer's own experience or from reading.

Even if you find essay writing difficult, after reading this book you should have a clear idea of what is expected and you should be able to write well enough to pass in any English language paper. Bare-pass essays are those that show an understanding of sentence structure, have few mechanical errors but perhaps lack the fluency of style, planning and originality of good prose. An examiner marks the essay paper on 'general impression' and uses his wide experience about the standard offered on subject matter, ideas, arrangement, vocabulary and descriptive techniques. The essay is a test of a candidate's ability to express his OWN opinions, experiences, impressions, feelings and interests. It is not a test of general knowledge or attitudes and the best work is usually written within your own experience.

The student must have plenty of practice in writing on a wide variety of topics. Learn to identify the different types of essays and find out which kind you can do best. Decide which types are in this book and attempt each yourself. Finally be critical of your work. Read it over and revise it carefully. This is never a waste of time.

1. Try to piece together your recollections of the days before you started school. [1 hour]

Plan.

1. Introduction — difficulty of remembering childhood.
2. Other children — cricket.
3. Sledging in winter.
4. Bicycles — personal incident.
5. Discovery of an old pram — its uses.
6. Prams, soapbox, uses — crash — pram broken.
7. Conclusion — school and change.

Looking back, childhood is like a series of snapshots contained in an album. One sees oneself in different guises at different times, but it is impossible to piece together everything that happened to form a continuous narrative. Early childhood is a series of images and highlights, linked by the slenderest threads.

There is a slight continuity. There were eight or ten other children who lived near us in the countryside. I was an only child but they used to play with me, partly because I had some of the best games equipment. My father had patiently made cricket stumps and bats and in summer we used to have large disorganised games. I used to bowl underarm and was fairly good, and remember knocking Ben's stumps out. One day an aunt gave us a cork cricket ball. At the end of the day Ben had a lump on his head, Eva, his sister, a year older than myself had lost a tooth, while I had a broken finger nail. My mother said she was glad we had lost the hard ball in some deep nettle beds and that in future we had to play with a sponge ball.

In winter we used to go sledging. Eva and I were the youngest and so were sent down the hill first to see if it was safe. Usually we fell off and got soaked, then the others would follow, simply to show that they were brave too. Occasionally, fights broke out because someone threw a snowball a bit too hard, or refused to drag a sledge back up the hill.

Bicycles and tricycles also took up a great deal of our time. When I was three someone gave me a child's two wheeled bicycle. All the others 'taught' me to ride. I did not hurt myself much by falling off until one day, when I could nearly ride. I was racing the older boys down a steep farm road, I wobbled, panicked, and pulled the front brake by mistake. I was in hospital three days with concussion and remember that the tribe came to see me, all looking clean, guilty and nervous. I was better in about a fortnight, but was scared for years when riding a bicycle downhill.

One summer, Eva and I found an old red pram. Everyone liked it. It had an iron frame with very few springs. In the autumn the pram became a chestnut transporter, and we once arrived back with it completely full. Then on a Saturday afternoon eight of us were riding down a hill in the pram when we crashed. None of us was hurt but the pram was damaged. Ben said he could repair it and everyone was keen to help, but there was little we could do as we had smashed the body work badly, but more disastrously we had smashed the axle. My father took the wheels off and made a soap box for us, which we could steer but it was not the same as having the pram to ride about in. The soapbox could only carry three people and it was not much good for dragging our own things about.

Finally, I went to school. At about that time other things changed rapidly. Two families left and the new people who came had children who were grown up — they were over twelve. Also Ben was nearly twelve by now so there was only Eva left to play with. Then she became interested in dolls and did not play cricket and climb trees and go sledging, so I was left to amuse myself.

2. The countryside in winter. **[45 min.]**

Plan.

1. Introduction — review of the seasons.
2. Relationships — town: country: winter.
3. Varieties of weather.
4. Snow.
5. Life in winter.

Winter is the most beautiful season of the year in the countryside. The harrassing days of March and April with their abrupt showers, the cold winds and bitter sunlight of May, the hot sunshine in June and July, the drab greens of August and over rich seasons of harvest and leaf fall in September and October give way to the gentle, cool months of early winter.

In the countryside, provided one is suitably dressed, fog, wind, rain, and snow are exhilarating and exciting. In the spring, summer and autumn leaves hide the true splendour of the countryside. Everything is overgrown. By contrast, in winter the trees are bare, the fields are ploughed and the light is ever changing.

Winter weather is varied. The most interesting skies are not found in summer. They are found in winter, when numerous cloud formations make kaleidoscopic patterns in the sky. The sun often shines through a haze creating a strange, ethereal world. When fog and frost combine, the morning sun shines meek yellow on to trees delicately iced as though by a band of mischevious pixies.

Snow is always exciting. Crisp frost and bright sunlight are blinding and dazzling. Animal tracks can be found. Some animals like foxes and badgers, can only be traced through the snow. Birds lose their instinctive fear of man when they are foraging for food and can be observed at close quarters. Drifts in the snow have a dramatic quality. They appear, like embryonic mountain ranges, along dykes and hedge banks. Icicle pendants hang from trees and cottages, ponds are crusted with silver grey ice mirrors.

Many people believe that everything is dead in winter, but this is a fallacy. Exciting species of birds appear; wild geese, on their migratory flights from the Arctic to Southern Europe silhouetted in the winter moonlight, wild duck, honking through the dusk sky, seek a patch of open water where they can land. If there is a prolonged snowfall, Scandinavian pigeons arrive in large flocks, and sit on the fields eating any green stuff they can find. There are also hordes of fieldfares and starlings.

Vegetation is unobtrusively present. In January incipient leaf buds begin to develop on the trees and snowdrops gently remind us of spring.

3. A seaside resort at night. [1 hour]

Plan

1. The Beach.
2. The sea.
3. Amusements.
4. The end of the night.

The sand is still warm, the tiny grains run in and out between one's toes. Children, the patient and tired donkeys, the boatmen with their 'trips round the bay, only fifty pence' cry have all gone. The little boy who spent the morning building a castle is asleep and the sea, silver under the summer moon, laps gently at its walls. The shrieks and laughs from a group of bathers float across the sands. A man throws a stick far out into the waves and his dog retrieves it, covering his master with salty spray. On the jetty, an angler baits his hook and waits.

The night sea is busy. Boatmen and fishermen prepare for the next day. Sparking plugs, carburrettors and nets receive careful attention. Heavy diesel engines pulsate softly in the dark as an inshore trawler noses its way out of the harbour for a lonely night's fishing a few miles offshore, its cabin and masthead lights glimmering faintly. Nets lie deep in the stern, while the helmsman in the dog cabin, a pipe in his mouth, gives his orders to the engineer. Out at sea are the lightships and marker buoys, stationary amongst the numerous moving lights of ships. Freighters and tramps, trawlers and liners pass quietly in the night. The rest of the harbour is still. Yachts, stripped of their sails, swing and yaw in the tidal currents, and softly bump together. Cabin cruisers are deserted, their owners being day time sailors only.

The strings of fairy lights illuminating the pier head, promenade and esplanade invite the visitor eager to lengthen his day. Shops, cafés and amusement arcades have their own neon lit attractions. Everything is larger than life. Cheap chrome glints a myriad flashes of colour, faded lampshades glow and jaded blondes acquire a new vivacity. Teenagers, middle aged couples, fathers and mothers pulling tired children make their way through the lighted streets. The place vibrates with noise, relaxing, care-erasing music, the rattle of coins, the clatter of one armed bandits and the monotonous calls of the bingo stall holders. Everyone is encouraged to spend money, as in the daytime, but there is a greater sense of urgency, as if the stall holders feel that another day is running out and tomorrow may bring storms and gales. The holidaymakers too are aware that another day in the seasonal fortnight has passed.

As the night wears on in the resort, small shopkeepers begin to put up the shutters. The funfair stops as numbers dwindle. Coffee bars and ice-cream parlours remain open to catch the last lingering trade. Dance halls are also late to close but last of all are the discotheques. As the first trawlers dock and the men set up the stalls for the morning fish auction, the last of the holidaymakers slowly wend their way to their hotels and lodgings. Only the litter blows low along the streets and even this will be gone by daybreak, swept up by the street cleaners or carried into the sea.

4. Your school is organising a function to which parents and friends are invited. Its purpose is to raise money for some new equipment, amenity or venture. Write a circular letter to parents and friends describing the function and explaining the project. [30 min.]

Plan.

1. Invitation.
2. Purpose of the events.
3. Contributions by the school.
4. Further contributions.
5. The dance.
6. Thanks for support.

Cumber House,
Bryar's Lodge,
Nettleton.

Dear Parent/Friend,

The pleasure of your company is requested at a garden fete and dance to be held at Cumber House in the afternoon and evening of Saturday 21st June.

These events are being organised by the school to aid our Oxfam efforts. As you may have read in the local press, the school is helping a fishing village on the shores of Lake Kariba. The funds over the last two years have been sufficient to buy the fishermen two motor launches and trawl nets. The aim of this venture is to raise money to donate another boat and to send two local long-shoremen to Africa for a year to advise the villagers how to handle trawl nets with which they are still unfamiliar.

Various departments of the school are taking part. In the afternoon, paintings, produced by the sixth form, and framed by the woodwork department, may be purchased. Foodstuffs and hand-made clothing will be offered by the Home Economics department. A magazine, written and edited under the auspices of the English department will be on sale. In it are full details of the activities and successes of the school in the last three years and it should be of special interest to former students.

The science and engineering departments have offered, for a small consideration, to carry out minor repairs to motor cars, irons, radios and tape recorders, so the fete will be an excellent opportunity to have household equipment repaired quickly and cheaply. Races and competitions for the younger children will be organised by the prefects. There will be a raffle, tombola and a shooting stall, round-abouts and swings. Tea will be available in the refectory, at a cost of 25 pence per head.

The dance will be held in the Great Hall, which, as school members know, leads to the veranda and lawns. If the night is fine, dancing will take place outside the school building. It starts at eight-thirty and tickets at £1.50 each may be obtained from the school secretary or any member of the Oxfam Committee.

We shall be grateful for your continued support to help those less fortunate than ourselves.

Yours sincerely,
J. N. Neagle.
[Head Boy: Scholarship VIth. Modern].

R.S.V.P.

5. Write a story entitled 'Never Again'. [1½ hours]

Plan.

1. Introduce character. Comments on his general abilities.
2. His special abilities.
3. Called in to effect a rescue.
4. Climbing the tree.
5. Kipling's joke.
6. Marooned.
7. Rescue.

Mrs. Eveling's Siamese cat, Kipling, was a splendid animal. In his youth she had taught him to play pussy ping pong and he could catch rats and mice with admirable dexterity. He had never been known to run away from any dog and all feared his long claws and unquestioned bravery. He did most of the things that a cat should do, keeping himself to himself, leading his own private life and bothering no one but his doting owner with the occasional request for food. He was fastidious, despised 'tinned food and would only eat best fillet of cod.

Perfect in every aspect but one, Kipling was the best cat north of the Humber-Mersey line. Regrettably he would climb trees. Occasionally he did this to catch birds, a cruel but understandable practice. More often he climbed trees to gain a better view of the surrounding countryside, for he was highly intelligent and appreciated scenic beauty. Locally, he held the record for sitting in a tree, and once spent seventy two hours meditating aloft. On that occasion I climbed up with bowls of milk and had patiently waited while he lapped them up. At the time I remarked that this seemed unwise because giving the cat waiter service would encourage him all the more to sit there. However, I accepted the seventy five pence that Mrs. Eveling gave me.

Having once put myself under obligation to both the cat and its mistress I was called in at the beginning of the next crisis. Kipling was up a tree, apparently fasting; he had been there for two and a half days. It was mid September and the equinox gales could be expected at any time. As I was the only inhabitant of less than forty in our village I was the only person considered agile enough to reach him. I agreed willingly, not knowing then that he was marooned forty-five feet up a wind buckled Douglas fir tree in full view in the centre of the village. By the time I did find out the position I was committed and pride drove me on.

I mounted the first twenty five feet on a ladder and wondered how Kipling had managed to run up the sheer, smooth trunk. My first problem came when I had to step into the branches of the tree. They all sloped downwards and creaked alarmingly. As I tried to keep my balance the ladder I had used to get this far fell to the ground. A curious crowd was already gathering below, faces upturned and fingers pointing. Everytime I got near the cat, he hopped up a few more branches and I followed. An opened tin of sardines, were of little help in enticing him [I did not know his strange culinary habits]. I would offer him a fish; he would swipe it from the ends of my finger and then hop up another two or three branches.

During the next hour and a half my admiration for Kipling turned to active dislike. From a distance he seemed the most friendly cat in the world, he purred and washed himself; but each time I came within six inches of him he became positively venemous —he spat and hissed at me and raked me with his claws. His green, deep set eyes gleamed: the cat was playing a practical joke and I was the victim. All the village was out now, cars had stopped, cameras clicked and people shouted advice. 'Grab him when he's not looking!' and 'watch you don't fall!' Finally, a blue and pink television truck arrived. I would probably be shown on 'Sportsview' as some new kind of activity.

No one seemed to know I was marooned. I wished that the tree was not swaying so much and wondered if it was safe as the parish council had feared that some of the trees were rotten. Finally, the fire brigade, telephoned as it later turned out by a cat lover, arrived. They need not have made so much noise over it. All that was needed was a good man with a long ladder but they came with a tender and water pump, ladder and a landrover and made a great show of moving everybody out of the way. Perhaps I should have to jump into a safety net I thought to myself. 'Climber, can you get down?' shouted a man with a megaphone. Lamely I shouted, 'I don't think so.' 'Stay there then!' It took another ten minutes for the lorry with the ladder to manoeuvre into position and Kipling watched the operation with bemused contentment.

Swaying alarmingly, the ladder poked its way towards me. A hardy young man was soon able to take me by the hand and help me on to it. Kipling, having had his pleasure nimbly descended the tree while I was still scrambling, pale and wan, down the ladder. They raised a cheer when I got down, the police wanted to know my name and address. Mrs. Eveling, with Kipling in her arms, kissed me. She cooed at the animal, 'My poor little Kippy. It's so nice to have friends to rescue us.' On the local newspaper they had ignored my comment, 'Never again!' and had inserted, 'Oh, yes', to the question, 'and would you go up the tree again for a cat?'

6. Describe a country which you have been to or which you have read about. **[1¼ hours]**

Plan

1. Topography of country.
2. Visible landscape.
3. Rural country — wildlife. Lapp tribesmen and reindeer.
4. Fishing and shooting.
5. Industry.
6. Importance of timber — for wood and paper exports.
7. Retention of national characteristics.
8. Life for the present day Finn.
9. Recreation.

The landscape of Finland is broken up into ridges and crests. Sixty thousand lakes have formed in occlusions in the ground and take up nine percent of the land area. Slightly bigger than the United Kingdom, there are 60,000 islands around the indented coast which make popular holiday resorts. In Helsinki there are nineteen hours of daylight in midsummer, whilst north of the Arctic Circle there are 73 days of sunlight and 53 days of constant darkness.

The landscape is mainly water and woodland. In the south west and along the south coast are deciduous and coniferous trees. Travelling north one passes through pine forests which peter out at the timber line formed by small birch trees. In the far north, the tundra, a mixture of rock and sparse grassland, lichens, and mosses, grow in the brief summer. In winter the whole country is blanketed with snow.

Primarily a rural country, depending on farming and forestry — often combined — Finland abounds with wild life. Fur bearing animals — red squirrel, musk rat, pine marten and fox — are common; twenty thousand wild elk still remain. The Lapps in the far north follow a way of life that has not changed for centuries. In summer they migrate to the highlands and north with their large herds of reindeer and in winter track back again to the timber line. Nomadic, the Lapps enjoy a freedom unparalleled in the rest of Europe, though the price they pay is a hard one — exposure to the winter storms and severe frosts.

In recent years the fish and game reserves have been widely advertised to attract tourists. Finland offers some of the best trout and salmon fishing and as a popular area with fishermen it will soon rank with Southern Ireland. For shooting enthusiasts there are grouse, wild duck, balk cock and ptarmigan.

There is industrialisation around Helsinki, the country's

capital. The worst effects of urbanisation, cramped streets, smoking factories and untidy sprawling towns have been avoided because of Finland's comparatively late industrial development. Planners, having seen the mistakes made in Britain, France and Germany, designed pleasant, well spaced towns with adequate parklands and recreation areas.

The basis of the economy is timber. Sawed, planed or mashed for wood pulp, it is the country's largest export. Throughout the country saw and planing mills abound. After the U.S.S.R., and Sweden, Finland is Europe's largest timber producing nation. Many of the forests are in the hands of small farmers who concentrate on lumber and dairy farming to make their livings.

Throughout a long history of invasion and foreign occupation [first the Swedes, then the French and finally the Russians] certain factors have contributed to the maintenance of Finnish hegemony. The national tongue is unique, being, besides Hungarian, the only Finno-Ugrian language in Europe. This language, comprised of many vowels and few consonants is suitable for folk art and poetry, and a thriving folk culture has existed for centuries in the country. Independent farmers — the Finns were never serfs — still keep alive the epic poetry, legends and stories. The National Museum in Helsinki contains the largest archives of folk lore and custom in the world. Museums throughout Finland—more than eighty of them—are often no less than models of earlier communities and settlements: they attest the strong pride that the people take in their heritage.

Life for the modern Finn is free and unhampered. Private enterprise is encouraged. At the same time adequate social insurance schemes and services exist. A small country, Finland realises the value of education. There are eight years compulsory education for all and this leads the young people to college, university or a trade school where they will learn the skills needed later in life.

Sport and music play a large part in the Finn's life. Weekly swims, even in winter, are taken after the weekly sauna bath. Winter sports like ice skating and skiing are popular and in 1964 Finns won the skiing events at the winter Olympics. Shooting is popular also. In 1935 and 1939 Finns were the world champions. Sibelius gained international acclaim as a musician. Two symphony orchestras give three concerts a week in Helsinki and the provinces. Each summer a week is devoted to the Sibelius music festival which ranks with those of Strasbourg and Edinburgh. For the tourist and visitor, Finland offers something all the year round.

7. A famous traitor in history or fiction. **[1½ hours]**

Plan.

1. Modern day November 5th.
2. The Reformation.
3. Hopes for a Roman Catholic Restoration.
4. Accession of James I of England, IV of Scotland.
5. Plot to kill sovereign and destroy Protestant leaders.
6. Guy Fawkes.
7. Preparations.
8. Discovery.
9. Arrest.
10. Torture and execution. Effect of plot on the Roman Catholic cause in England.

Children eagerly anticipate November 5th, the annual commemoration of the Guy Fawkes' plot to blow up the Houses of Parliament. Old age pensioners and animals are terrified from mid September onwards as irresponsible youths let off fireworks prematurely. On the night itself there are always numerous reports of accidental burnings and maimings. However, most people luckily enjoy themselves and come to no harm. Parties are often held around bonfires with roast potatoes and roast chestnuts. There is usually a sense of disappointment as the dummy effigy of Guy Fawkes is enveloped by the flames. Weeks of collecting and bonfire building and weeks of pocket money are consumed within an hour or two.

Few know who Guy Fawkws was, except that he tried to blow up Parliament. However, the plot that is so lightly commemorated every November was a serious affair. It took place in 1604. To fully understand one has to go back to the Reformation of 1534-38. In these years Henry VIII declared himself head of the Church of England, and ordered the desecration of various tombs of Roman Catholic Saints. In Canterbury Cathedral, Thomas a Becket's tomb was destroyed and jewels, embedded in the monument were seized. These alone amounted to a present day value of three million pounds. Church lands were seized. Roman Catholics were fined and the Monasteries closed and pulled down.

Many people suffered harshly and many hoped to see a Roman Catholic Reformation. Plots were rife. Rebellion in the sixteenth century was usually associated with the religious problems. A brief return to Roman Catholicism was made under the regime of 'Bloody Mary', who vigorously persecuted Protestants in the years 1550-1555. With the accession of Elizabeth I there was a return to Protestantism or Anglicanism. While spies for both sides travelled the country and recusants [Roman Catholics] fled to the continent or suffered in England, no really dangerous plots came to light, such was the iron hand with which Elizabeth and her ministers ruled. Even so, towards the end of her reign one aristocrat, the young Earl of Essex led a serious rebellion for the Catholic cause thwarted only at the last minute.

With the accession of James I of England and IV of Scotland, Roman Catholics hoped for better treatment. Not unnaturally they sought entry to the professions from which they had been barred. Again, relief from the heavy fines was one of their aims. Unluckily for the rank and file of the Roman Catholics, James was vexed in February 1604 by the threat of rebellion. He stopped his characteristic equivocations and supported the Anglicans. All Roman Catholic Clergy were expelled. In August several priests were hanged because they had dallied too long. Meanwhile, some men were considering how to take action in the Houses of Parliament.

The plotters knew that if they were to succeed in their extreme action they had not only to dispose of the King but the leading Protestants also. For even without a sovereign it was unlikely that men who owed their wealth to the 'new' religion would take a Roman Catholic power bid kindly. In some ways the plot was unique: only men of 'name and blood' were employed. None of the usual cut-throats and footpads—frequent in those days—seems to have had a part. Throughout the country influential landowners, faced with ruin and hoping for preferment backed the plot. Admittedly they were very reluctant to give active support: they would still have to live in England after the plot and no one was to tell how it would turn out.

Probably few of them knew of Guy Fawkes in the summer of 1604. He was a Yorkshireman who had fought for the English Catholic Legion in Flanders. He was brought into the plot because he had a practical knowledge of tunnelling, gained from experience in operations against the Dutch when he had burrowed under their lines, planted gunpowder and exploded their trenches. Fawkes was no reluctant hero: he was himself a fanatic and it was largely due to him that satisfactory progress was made. If everyone had been as dedicated as Fawkes the plot might have succeeded.

Luck also helped, for the plotters were able, under Fawkes's direction, to hire a building in Parliament itself. One day Fawkes, in his tunnelling had heard a rumbling, had investigated and had discovered that it was a woman moving sacks of sea coal in a room beneath the House of Lords. This room was later to carry the charges for the final explosion. In all, thirty six barrels of gunpowder were placed in the vaults of Parliament. Roman Catholic circles were informed and there were some, notably the Jesuits, who would have called off the plot. As it was, the leading Jesuits in London fled, fearing the consequences. Meanwhile the powder was laid and primed, and iron bars were placed on the barrels to act as missiles with which to crack the roof.

Discovery of the plot was due to Tresham, once an angry young man but at the time of the plot an influential landowner with friends in the House of Lords. He sought to warn them not to attend Parliament and hoped that this would not betray the plot. Soon it was apparent that the plans were known and action was being taken. No arrests would have been made as the conspirators were unknown to the authorities. However, Fawkes's allies gave themselves away by trying to raise rebellion in the countryside whilst Fawkes himself lingered on hoping to make a coup single handed.

On the afternoon of 4th November he waited outside Parliament, despite the fact that the guards had been alerted. His vigil, during which he awaited his chance, was finally broken at eleven at night when a group of strange men approached him, seized him, examined the faggots he was carrying and after a vicious struggle overpowered him. It is recorded that he was tied up with his own garters. News of his arrest spread quickly and most of the súpporters of the rebellion sensibly lay low. There was no possibility of anyone coming forward to aid Fawkes.

Fawkes paid the price for his anarchy to the full. In a period of English history when torture was formally acknowledged as a means to obtain evidence he was punished unmercifully. Gradually he revealed the whole plot. On February 1, 1606 he was carried to the executioner's gibbet, being too weak to walk after his ordeal. With him died the last real hope for the Roman Catholics in Britain until the nineteenth century. His plot aroused the contempt and fear of the mob and indicated to the country landowners that rebellion in the interest of religion had fearful consequences for anyone who failed. A final footnote may be added, Fawkes, for all his plotting would have failed. Modern ballistics experts have calculated that the amount of gunpowder available would have done little more than create clouds of stinking smoke. It would perhaps have smashed some masonry but no more. Certainly the Houses of Parliament would not have been rent atwain.

8. Write a letter to the editor of your local newspaper, setting out your views on a proposal to ban smoking in places of entertainment. [30 min.]

Plan.

1. Introduction.
2. Freedom of the smoker.
3. Health factors.
4. Social factors.
5. Case for ban being made.

'The Gables',
Wayside Close,
Long Sutton,
Surrey.
4th October, 1978.

The Editor,
'Evening News',
City Centre,
Long Sutton.

Dear Sir,

In view of the acrimonious and emotive correspondence that has appeared in your columns over the Watch Committee's proposal to ban smoking in public places I feel obliged to state my views. I shall begin by taking up some of the points already made on this issue.

The gentleman who wrote about the 'democratic rights of the British smoker' and saw the Watch committee's proposals as 'a Fascist gesture by those in power to curb the pleasures of the decent man' seems to understand little of either fascism or democracy. Political labels only confuse the issue and lead to irrelevance. His letter was about freedom, but surely the question must arise of 'freedom for whom, and from what?' It is not only the smoker's freedom that is being challenged: the non-smoker similarly has a freedom and should not be forced to accept smoking indiscriminately in public places.

Stalemate is quickly reached in arguments about the democratic rights of smokers and non-smokers. The health factor is a sounder reason for banning smoking. Medical research has indicated that smoking is detrimental to health and may cause or aggravate lung cancer, bronchial complaints, and stomach troubles. Many addicts claim that there is a compensating quality about it for they suggest that cigarettes soothe the nerves. However, the evidence for this is scanty. If smoking harms a smoker it should be discouraged, for an invalid is a liability to the country and may cost many thousands of pounds to treat. Also, non-smokers should not be exposed to the irritants and possible diseases that can be caused by cigarette smoking in public places.

Smoking is sometimes advocated as a social asset. The offer of a cigarette is used to soothe the opening of a conversation: it makes people relaxed and at ease, and it gives people something to do with their hands. Smoking has its own rituals and paraphernalia. But the dropping of ash and subsequent damage to floors and furnishings, the de-tarring of pipe bowls and the spattering of spittle are not desirable social graces.

More important than this is the fire hazard and many have died because of the carelessly discarded match or cigarette butt.

Thus, there is a good case for banning smoking in the interests of the public. Smoking amongst children and young people should also be discouraged, and the Watch Committee's decision must be upheld.

Yours faithfully,

A former addict.

9. Describe your thoughts during a walk at night. [30 min.]

Plan.

1. My thoughts on the place.
2. My thoughts on the surroundings.
3. The atmosphere.
4. The town.
5. The steel community.

Whitehill Lane, on the outskirts of the town, has no lighting. As I walked, the moonlight outlined the antennae of television aerials. Trees, denuded by the recent frosts, raised spectral fingers to the starlit sky. Little wonder that the ancients endowed the moon and the night sky with magical properties and no surprise that poets have made the heavens a subject for mystic speculations and metaphysical verse. With thoughts of my own nothingness in the giant scheme of the universe I plodded on.

I knew the road well. In another ten minutes I would have left the last suburban outpost, would have crossed a stile and would be climbing a steep slope. From a high vantage point I would be able to survey the city, stretching out for nine miles along the river valley. I knew I would be alone.

The headlights of a car lit up the hillside and two red malevolent dots peered at me from the darkness. Ahead was clearly the devil or a bullock. I heard the animal's snorts and decided to make a wide detour. The hillside gave way to dead bracken and fern, and moisture penetrated my heavy denims. An owl shrieked, perhaps one of the lost souls who wandered the world in search of peace.

I walked as far as I could before I gave in to the temptation to look back at the town. The curtains had long been drawn. I thought of children, pyjamed and blanketed, husbands damping down fires, spinsters sipping their night-caps. Red and green neon signs still flashed their advertising messages but I did not think they would find a ready market now.

Six miles away the coking ovens and blast furnaces threw up a shower of metal cutting scarlet semi-circular arcs into the night sky. This was another community with its white molten master from which poured security in the weekly wage packet.

All this was supposed to represent power and progress. But alone on the hillside I felt apart, as of another age.

10. A violent storm or blizzard has occurred in the area where you live. Compose a report for a local newspaper about its effects on transport and communications. [30 min.]

Plan

1. Severity of blizzard.
2. Survey by helicopter.
3. Breakdown of telegraph lines.
4. Effect in the town.
5. Advice on the use of existing communications.

SEVEREST BLIZZARD ON RECORD

Yesterday's blizzard, which lasted for seventeen hours was unprecedented for its severity. The meteorological office had issued snow and gale warnings but few people could have judged the true nature of the storm. Seven inches of snow fell and gusts reached hurricane force.

At early dawn, as the winds subsided, I joined one of the helicopter crews about to determine the extent of the damage. Everything was shrouded in snow. All shapes were muted; river, field and road were one. Here and there a black tree branch protruded and a small group of animals struggled pathetically and hopelessly in a shifting drift. Occasionally, someone waved frantically from the upstairs window of an isolated farmhouse. The location of these were mapped so that medical help, food and warm clothing could be dropped later.

Power line and telegraph cables have been blown down or collapsed under the weight of snow and news is scrappy. The Electricity Board and G.P.O. are, as yet, unable to estimate when they can repair all the damage. The local M.P., Mr. . . . . . is seeking to bring a motion before the House of Commons, declaring a disaster area, and requesting the help of the army.

No trains, buses or cars reached town yesterday, while in town itself, fallen trees and overturned cars made many hundreds late for work. In view of the absenteeism, two of the largest factories in the town have closed. At another two, workers left for home, claiming that it was impossible to work without heating. Several gas pipes have been fractured and inhabitants have been warned not to use gas appliances.

Warnings that there will be further snow falls during the night and that ground and air frost will be widespread have been given. Every effort is being made during the present lull to contact people cut off in outlying districts and helicopters are dropping bales of hay to starving flocks of sheep and herds of cattle. People are asked to use the post office and telephone services as infrequently as possible, for unnecessary calls may hold up important and urgent messages.

11. Describe the scene in an examination room. [45 min.]

Plan

1. The room at the beginning of the examination.
2. During the examination.
3. During the examination.
4. The end of the examination.

The great hall is filled to capacity with rows of neat desks each with its examination number, freshly filled inkwell and white unsullied blotting paper. The white painted stage topped front centre with the green and gold school crest is closed by its green drop curtains. The long windows to the right of the hall look out on grass tennis courts and to the left of the hall is a rose garden and a busy road. The students enter quietly; the girls in their white blouses and green skirts, the boys in white shirts and grey trousers. Their faces are subdued with anxious expectancy. The invigilator in his black gown walks between the desks handing out foolscap books and giving instructions. The Principal ostentatiously breaks the seal on the envelope containing the question papers and hands half the batch to the invigilator. The papers are placed face downwards on the desks and all are waiting for 'you may begin'.

Some candidates start scribbling immediately, feverishly anxious to write what they know before they forget; others sit poised and thoughtful, planning their answers. The door opens noisily and a boy breathless from his sprint up the corridor, enters. 'Sorry I'm late, Sir'. Disapprovingly, the invigilator points to an empty desk and blushing, the lad stumbles awkwardly to his place.

The clock ticks relentlessly, the supervisor a little bored and tired, settles himself more comfortably at his vantage point. A secretary brings him coffee which he sips perfunctorily. After an hour most candidates are working steadily, writing, calculating or re-reading questions. A young girl near the front dangles her pen lightly between her fingers and gazes miserably at the question paper. The invigilator studiously ignores the unspoken plea in the hunched up shoulders. A boy gathers up his papers and head held defiantly high stalks out of the hall. The tantalizing smell of steak and kidney pie wafts up from the kitchen and someone's stomach gurgles, complaining because it had no breakfast. Through the open windows comes the hum of traffic and the laughter of the rest of the school enjoying its mid morning break. Somewhere a bell rings and silence is restored outside.

At last the examination period draws to an end. One candidate whiles away the last ten minutes drawing circles on the back of the question paper. Feet shuffle and papers are rustled restlessly.

'Please check that your name and number are on the front of your answer books and that all questions are numbered correctly.' The invigilator stirs languidly, his voice suggests the unlikelihood of his directions being followed. There is a slight pause then, 'Stop writing please. Leave your papers on the desks'. Within ten minutes the hall is empty. Quickly, the papers are collected in numerical order and checked and packed in envelopes to be despatched to the examiners. The blotting paper is sorted and the rows of desks tidied for the next examination.

12. Maps and map makers. [45 min.]

Plan.

1. Elements of map making.
2. Medieval maps.
3. Voyages made with these ancient maps.
4. Mercator. Beginning of modern cartography.
5. Present day maps.
6. Skills needed to use a map. Journeys.

Cartographic skill is equated with a sound knowledge of mathematics and the precise use of accurate measuring instruments. However, ancient tribes have demonstrated their skill at drawing rudimentary maps and early explorers achieved good results with these. The first Arctic explorers used simple maps drawn by Eskimos. Similarly, South Sea Islanders possessed cane charts which helped early navigators in the Pacific. Spanish Conquistadores were aided in the Mexican invasion by the maps of the semi-literate Indians. Again, the Egyptians had useable maps and Ptolemy used them when compiling his work 'Geography'.

In the Middle Ages, advanced thinkers who suspected that the earth might be round encountered opposition from the Heads of the Church who argued that such a doctrine was unscriptural. Because of this, medieval maps show the known world to be surrounded by water. Maps were either rectangular, circular or oval; Paradise was the Far East. The best maps of the time were prepared by the Arabs. Marco Polo and Vasco da Gama found maps of the Indian Ocean which were serviceable.

Using elementary maps, the fifteenth and sixteenth century navigators sailed around the world. Errors of up to thirty degrees in longitudinal plots were common. Also the magnetic north pole and its variation led to further errors. It is scarcely surprising that foundering and shipwreck were common and that five out of six sailors on voyages of exploration lost their lives.

The first accurate maps for known regions were those prepared by Mercator and published after his death in 1595. At this time Antwerp and Amsterdam were the most advanced map making centres in the world, as Portugal had been a century before. Nations with large maritime fleets acknowledged the saving that accurate charts could make. By the eighteenth century, increased shipping tonnage gave further impetus to map making, and here France excelled in combining travellers' tales and cartographers' mathematical skills. Modern cartographic surveys really started in the mid eighteenth century. The Ordnance Survey was founded in 1791. In 1825 the six inch to the mile map of England and Ireland was undertaken and by 1891 a proposal that the world be mapped on the same scale was put forward and adopted at a conference in Berne.

Now maps for all conceivable purposes and in all forms exist and considerable artistry is displayed in many of them. Very modern Atlases sometimes take the form of aerial photographs. It is proposed to use these extensively in school teaching in the future as they are easier to interpret than diagrammatic sketches.

Despite the skill of the map maker, the map user has to display certain simple skills also. Because people often make mistakes with maps they develop a deep distrust of them. Occasionally, the apocryphal remark, 'the map must be wrong' is heard from harrassed hikers, scouts and school cadets. With imagination, however, the map becomes an energetic man's window on adventure.

13. Discuss a book that you have read. [1 hour]

Plan.

1. Author.
2. Dog.
3. Qualities of book.
4. Exploration of New England.
5. Canadian Border.
6. Chicago.
7. 'The Badlands'.
8. Montana.
9. California.
10. Desert. Texas.
11. Deep South.
12. Race for home.

John Steinbeck, internationally famous novelist and Nobel Peace Prize winner, discovered that after spending many years abroad he no longer knew his own country. He set out, therefore, with a large French poodle as his travelling companion, to re-explore the continent. He travelled in a commercial truck, converted to a dormobile, and he hoped it would be sufficient. The living quarters of 'Rocinante', his vehicle, were designed like the cabin of a ship. His experiences are recorded in his book, 'Travels with Charley in Search of America'.

His companion is worthy of a few words. The dog proved to be an effective night watchman, although, as the author pointed out, Charley was ineffective in attacking anyone. Proverbially, the animal's bark was much worse than his bite. Steinbeck's interest was as much with the people he met as with the places he saw. The dog was very good at gaining introductions for the traveller, for people proved very eager to talk, once they had encountered the dog. To allay suspicion as to his identity Steinbeck took a couple of rifles with him and told those he met that he was on a hunting trip. Few recognised him and so people talked to him without knowing that their words would be memorably recorded.

The meetings with people, combined with the graphic description of the different regions give the book its strength. 'Travels with Charley. . .' is not a traditional travelogue with long passages describing the different states and cities he saw. Instead, Steinbeck recorded that which interested him and which he felt would sustain a reader. He admits that there may be bias in the book, but if there is, this does not discount the lively way in which his journey is presented.

Tracking north from New York he explored the New England

States first. At times one felt that he could be writing about parts of Wales or Scotland, for the scenery is much the same. Some significant differences do appear however. Although a sporting hunter himself Steinbeck was appalled at the trigger happy business men he saw or sensed shooting at anything that moved as they enjoyed an autumn holiday in 'the sticks.' Critically Steinbeck commented on the radio broadcasts which warned people not to blow their noses with a white handkerchief in case a gunman mistook the white for the tail of a deer and took a shot.

On the Canadian border the exit and entry laws of the United States came in for criticism as Charley lacked the correct innoculation certificates and would cause trouble when Steinbeck wanted to recross the border. In circumstances akin to those of a Brian Rix farce Steinbeck satisfied officialdom and continued his journey. Leaving Canada he travelled to Chicago where he met his wife. Again, his visit to one of the city's great hotels led to a humorous debâcle when the manager feared that Steinbeck, in his traveller's clothes might adversely affect hotel trade. However, he was an old customer and prominent public figure so he could not be thrown out. Eventually the author was temporarily accommodated in a room used by someone else. In his emergency accommodation he analysed the débris of a private party left from the night before and passed some revealing comments about the behaviour of people when they think no one knows who they are.

Having met his wife and having spent a few days with her, Steinbeck travelled on across America. It was after Chicago that he came to what may be called the true America. After Chicago the large industrial towns of the American mid-west appeared, great sprawling conurbations with a multitude of traffic signs which terrorised and confused the author. Caravan sites were frequently found and some people spent their whole lives on these. As one van dweller explained to Steinbeck a home on wheels gave absolute freedom. If a man was sacked or became redundant he could move on. There was no commitment to stay in one place. Steinbeck, author of the eloquent protest novel 'The Grapes of Wrath' had once sprung to the defence of the displaced people from Oklahoma who had trekked to California in the nineteen twenties and thirties. He had felt then that people should have roots. In the nineteen sixties he found that these were considered a disadvantage. He accepted this —much against what he thought were the inborn loyalties of Americans.

Moving from the industrial mid-west to the true west of the 'Badlands' home of Indians, coyotes and uncooperative small farmers who would not give him directions, the haste and rush of modern life came in for criticism. Steinbeck, surprisingly was not a good driver and hated to find himself harrassed amongst heavy traffic. In St. Pauls he actually crossed the Mississippi twice according to his map, seeing the river on neither occasion.

Only in Montana did the narrator feel that he had discovered the old and traditional America. Local dialects and customs still remained. There was a certain cynicism and criticism over politics. People said what they thought and would not be quizzed. Here the values of the frontiersman and pioneer remained.

New towns, larger roads, plastic and formica service areas had become well established features of Steinbeck's commentary when he reached his home state of California. Like everyone else he had known that, since 1945, there had been a move towards the west coast. Even then he could hardly believe the transformations which had occurred. Seattle, a small compact city in his childhood, had become a massive sprawl, creeping up the hillsides. Hilltops had been levelled to house radio stations. Untamed woodlands had been torn down and drained to site factories. In his home town he argued about politics with his sister and found his fame was an embarrassment to the people he had once known.

He left California, preferring to retain his earlier memories and recrossed the Rockies to drive across the deserts of Arizona to reach the 'pan handle' of Texas. At this stage in the book the vastness and the regional variety of America strikes one very strongly. A few weeks and chapters before, driving through New England, he had worried about the early snow falls: in Arizona he was concerned about the effect of the sun on Charley. In Texas he visited some ranching friends and found that they were very much as they are portrayed in films. There, he felt the odd man out where the talk was about cars, cattle and horses. Around him he saw the nonchalance that great wealth carries with it and he was pleased to be on his way.

Always a social critic, racial violence in the deep south disgusted him. He saw a small negro girl being shouted and jeered at as state troopers led her into a newly desegregated school. Steinbeck himself was stopped by the police from taking 'Rocinante' too close to the trouble area in case anyone seeing the New York number plates attacked him. In the deep south New Yorkers were seen as liberals and trouble makers. The attitude of mind underlining racial violence was well summarised in the thirty year old southern white whom Steinbeck picked up as a hitchiker and who explained the ethos behind the colour bar and 'nigger hatred'. Before he had time to say much however, Steinbeck had stopped the van and had forcibly ejected him.

Suddenly the narrator realised that his long journey was over for him. He was no longer interested in the route he was following. Instead he wanted to be back in New York and in his home on one of the Staten Island waterfronts. He briefly described his dash home, covering vast mileages. The great journey for Steinbeck was over and the great excitement for the reader is concluded at this stage. However, at the end of the book one feels a much deeper knowledge of America than when the book began, for the search has been a successful as well as a fruitful one.

14. Travel in an earlier century. [1¼ hours]

Plan.

1. Travel regarded as an essential part of education.
2. Problems.
3. Journeys on unmade roads.
4. Plague and other diseases.
5. Thieves.
6. Foreign travel.
7. Piracy.
8. Religious upheavals.
9. Mainly young who travelled.

Wealthy, established parents in the sixteenth century believed that travel was essential to their sons' proper education. Some men, like the youthful Sir Philip Sidney, charmed the intellectual and scholarly circles of Europe. Others, like the eldest son of William Cecil, dissipated themselves in riotous living, disgracing both themselves and their families. However, all young voyagers were sent on their way with high minded advice. The Earl of Rutland was told:

> 'Your study must be of what use to make your travel . . . . your lordship shall see the beauty of many cities, and learn the language of many nations. But your lordship must look further than these for the greatest beauty is the inward ornament of the mind'.

Cautioned thus, young travellers made the preliminaries to setting out. Large baggage trains usually accompanied them, and a number of outriders rode on ahead as guards and guides. Horses had to be hired sometimes for as much as ten shillings a day. If someone wanted to go abroad they had to obtain government permission, for the Tudors were constantly on the watch for spies and infiltrators from Roman Catholic countries. However, many clandestine journeys must have been made in the century for respectable voyagers, commenting on their travels often tell of once well to do families living the life of recusant refugees abroad.

Having gathered baggage and permits together the journey could begin. The roads were rough and badly maintained; everyone was supposed to spend six days a year repairing them but few did so. Instead they shirked their duties and let the adventurous fare as best they could through potholes floods and oozing mud. Roads were supposed to be fifty feet wide, but chronicle accounts indicate that land shortage had reduced many to a mere twenty or twelve feet wide. Journeys were uncomfortable, and injury could come from many quarters. One woeful gentleman wrote that he was detained in Newcastle because a horse having almost trod off the nail of his big toe made it extemely painful to even hobble.

Other hazards faced the traveller. Plague and influenza were serious illnesses and the areas where they occurred were best avoided. Again, a traveller, in an age of bad communications could never know if he was about to run into a trouble spot where riots might be taking place. In 1538, 1549, the 1560's and 1590's serious disturbances took place. Some were on grounds of religion, some over food shortages and agrarian enclosures and some over unemployment in the cloth industry. Any traveller, with the proper trappings of a well established person could be attacked. Even Elizabeth the First was once surrounded by a mob of ragged hooligans in Islington.

Besides men with a genuine grievance, there were countless 'sturdy rogues and vagabonds'. The Dissolution of the Monasteries, the Tudor coinage debasements, and chronic unemployment impoverished many people. Often the only recourse was to take to the roads and live as best they could. Thus young men formed themselves into armed gangs to rob the rich travellers. So it was that the Earl of Bedford almost lost the gold christening cup he was taking to the future James VI. Many notable families suffered in this way and to safeguard themselves they rode with all haste from inn to inn. Often lunch on the road consisted of no more than a pickled herring or an orange, eaten while still in the saddle. Cantering on a gelding—the popular steed of the century—over unmade roads could have only suited those sound of wind and limb, and keen of eye.

Foreign travel was the most hazardous of all. Ships leaked alarmingly and winds were often contrary. Food was poor and scanty. Henry Sidney, on his way to take up a post in Ireland, spent two months and lost fifteen hundred pounds worth of household utensils and his wine, as well as a faithful servant, coasting up and down the Welsh coast because of adverse winds. Any traveller going abroad also had to take his horses with him and these, crowded on a small deck, used to smell insufferably.

Piracy outstripped all these perils however. The west country ports abounded with English privateers who, Elizabeth I told the Spanish ambassador, were Scottish pirates speaking English as a disguise. Predatory, they impartially robbed English and foreign alike. Similarly, the 'hell hounds of Dunkirk' commanded the approaches to the continent. One prominent Privy Councillor arrived in Dover from a Channel crossing dressed only in his shirt. Pirates had taken all his other possessions.

Once abroad, the adventurer had to be careful and his choice of countries was limited. Italy was out because it was Roman Catholic and from there came all the sins in the world. Men who returned from Italy were, in Harrison's view, 'far worse men than they went out'. France was looked on askance. 'It was a nation which was enough to vex any man, so unstable, so uncertain, impudent, unfaithful and ever inclining to the worst'. The countries considered respectable were the decided Protestant countries and this left the dank regions of the Benelux countries and the Netherlands. Without putting too fine a point on it, these countries were not the most entrancing in Europe.

Perhaps in view of all the hardships, bother and danger Englishmen preferred to stay at home. A few hardy men like Drake and his crew sailed round the world, and some merchants ventured to the Middle East, the Baltic and Russia but the majority only made efforts to travel when they were forced to do so. The longest sufferers of all were perhaps the soldiers, who, in enhancing the greater glory of the Elizabethan monarchy, had to march many miles. These men had not even the minimum comforts of the normal traveller. Understandably, the greatest desire of the ex-patriate Englishman at this time was to return to his native land.

15. Describe the buildings you would see driving through your home town. [30 min.]

Plan.

1. Entrance to the town from the south.
2. The centre of the town.
3. Leaving the town.
4. The outskirts of the town.

Our town has the advantages of being near to the sea and to some of the most beautiful countryside in the land. The road into the town from the south follows the coastline. On the one side are the dunes, sand and sea. On the other side, one drives first through an area of ribbon development, 1920 suburban villas, each with its architectural idiosyncracies; mock Tudor, sham Georgian, American square frame and split level bungalows. The University has been enlarged and added to so that the campus now comes down to the road. The Town hall on the left is a white square building and during the war it had to be camouflaged with green paint. Rounding a treacherous right hand bend, followed a few yards further on by an equally hazardous left hand bend, one first sees the town's splendid Norman Church, unfortunately dwarfed by the power station and its triple stack of cooling towers.

In the town centre is a large covered market, medieval in design and disastrously 'restored' by the Victorians and the blue roof is now smudged with soot. The High Street has been almost completely rebuilt and modernised. Boutiques, departmental stores, furniture shops and supermarkets line each side of the street. All have square windows filled with colourful well displayed merchandise. At the end of the High Street, opposite the Railway Station is the Grand Hotel. Its revolving doors lead to a world of red carpeted four star luxury.

Through the traffic lights and on—the shops are smaller, dark and dingy. The road passes through rows of large Victorian houses, with steps leading up to them. A hundred year's industrial grime has bitten into their facade giving a drab uniformity. Two window boxes supporting anaemic looking asters perch precariously on a second storey window ledge, a pathetic attempt at gaiety. Only the shell of an age of grandeur remains. The many doorbells show that the large rooms are now divided into flats. The town is growing out of itself. Some of the old houses are being pulled down exposing walls with flaking, flowery wall paper and intricately worked fire grates. Flowers grow on the broken stonework and parts have been cleared by the council for use as car parks. Some of the scars are hidden by advertising hoardings.

On the outskirts of the town the road passes the tall sombre walls of the jail, then by-passes the new industrial estate. Here the buildings are functional, square blocks, cylindrical towers, tall chimneys. Then under the railway bridge, past the gas works and out to the open road. Now there are only the fields and the trees.

16. Give an account of the life of a famous scientist. [1 hour]

Plan.

1. Isaac Newton. Childhood.
2. Failure at farming.
3. Cambridge.
4. Return home. First mathematical discoveries.
5. Telescope.
6. Gravity.
7. Simple life at Cambridge.
8. Edmund Halley.

Isaac Newton, a premature baby, was not expected to live. Born in 1642, the year of Galileo's death, he lived until 1727. In this time great scientific advances were made, many of which stemmed from Newton's own work. His childhood revealed little of the fame that his genius was to bring. His father died before he was born, and Isaac was brought up with his grandparents. At twelve he was sent from the Lincolnshire village of Woolsthorpe to Grantham school. He did little work and was regarded as idle. Most of his time was spent in making windmills for a little girl, daughter of the family with whom he lodged. It is recorded that he unintentionally terrorised drunken yokels because he flew kites at night with small lamps attached to their tails. At sixteen his mother took him from school to run the family farm when her second husband had died.

At farming Newton was a total failure. He lacked initiative and interest. Each week when the cart was loaded with wares for the Grantham market Newton and an aged farm servant travelled with it. Sometimes in Grantham, Newton left all the family business of buying and selling in the hands of the old man and took himself off to the local chemist's shop where he read scientific books. Realizing that he was unsuited to farming his mother sent him back to school and for the first time he began to show that he had ability in academic subjects.

In 1661 he went to Trinity College, Cambridge. He paid for his tuition by working as a servant for one of the tutors. At first he studied Greek, Latin and Mathematics. His tutors recognised no exceptional ability in the young student. Then the eminent Classicist, Isaac Barrow, transferred from the Chair of Greek to that of Mathematics. With a mind comparable in intellectual ability to Newton's, Barrow encouraged the talented young man. At the age of twenty two Newton took his Bachelor Degree.

Plague epidemics in the following year, 1665, caused Newton to return to his home village. At Woolsthorpe he made some of his notable discoveries. He developed a method for differential and integral calculus, a problem which had been teasing the minds of Pascal, Barrow and Willis. He also found a solution to the problem posed by the area of the parabola and worked his answer out to fifty two decimal places. In addition he worked on the binomial theorem and the general method of expression of algebraical functions in infinite series.

With these solid achievements behind him, he turned his creative, scientific mind to telescopes and, adapting an earlier idea, succeeded in building a reflecting telescope. Eventually he presented a model to the Royal Society and was made a fellow in 1772.

For a number of years he had been preoccupied with the problem of gravity. Galileo had sought to prove that the greater the distance between two objects the smaller the attraction beween them. Hence, while a small object thrown into the air will fall to the ground, the moon, because of its distance away from the earth, does not fall on to the earth. The crucial problem was in deciding what the accurate measurements of the earth were, and for Newton, as well as for Galileo, much of the work was speculative. However, in 1672 Picard published tables which gave much more accurate estimates of the earth's circumference than had previously been available. From these Newton worked and succeeded in obtaining a serviceable theory of gravitation. However, he refrained from publishing, because of his shy and modest character.

One of the reasons for Newton's achievement was undoubtedly the simple way in which he lived. He had returned to Cambridge after the plague epidemic and in 1669 gained the Professorship in Mathematics when Barrow resigned. This brought him a salary of £200 a year with a work load of fifty conferences and twenty four lectures. His lectures became models and the talented young man was brought to the attention of Charles II. patron of the Arts and Sciences. Success brought with it enemies. Newton wrote a paper on the spectrum and found himself attacked by Robert Hooke, experimenter to the Royal Society. Hooke claimed that Newton had lifted the ideas from a paper he himself had written in 1665. Newton, rather than face public embarrassment, offered to resign from the Royal Society, but other, impartial men realised that Newton's paper was his own work, for Hooke could not support his allegations with sound mathematics.

Fame was brought to the modest Newton by the intervention of the young astronomer, Edmund Halley. Halley had sought information on the movement of the planets and had already approached Hooke, Wren and the Royal Society. They could not help him, so he visited Newton, who not only solved Halley's immediate scientific problem but settled many other issues which had caused dissent and discussion amongst physicists. Halley knew Newton's work was important and persuaded him to publish. In fifteen months Newton wrote 'Principia Naturalis', a work which deduced the general movement of the planets and outlined the laws of gravity. The Royal Society was impressed with this work, but could not find the money necessary to publish it. Neither could Newton, so Halley himself published the book in 1687 and Newton was immediately acclaimed in intellectual circles for what he was —a genius.

The strain of long years of work was beginning to wear Newton down. One day he left a candle burning in his room, and several original scientific papers were burned. The great researcher became moody and despondent. However, he proved resilient and was cheered when in 1694 he was offered a post as Warden of the Mint. This carried with it a large salary, and gave Newton another opportunity to show his capabilities. Challoner, the prince of forgers, aided by several prominent politicians, soon fell a victim to Newton's detective methods. Similarly the whole administrative procedure was revised under the direction of Newton's incisive mind.

Success bred success and Newton was appointed Master of the Mint, with a salary of two thousand pounds a year. In 1703 he resigned his chair of Mathematics at Cambridge. He became President of the Royal Society and in 1705 was knighted. He continued working until the time of his death in 1727.

17. Tell the story of how you came upon a scene of desolation.
[1 hour]

Plan.

1. Shepperton.
2. Yellow lorries.
3. Looking at the village again.
4. Road to farm.
5. New development.
6. The mining complex.
7. The river.

Shepperton was a Dorchester village where nothing had happened since the monastery had been pulled down in the Reformation. There were few jobs for the young and it had become a place where old people lived. A few farm labourers, over the centuries, had been the only inhabitants in the dilapidated thatched cottages. For a population of four hundred and fifty nine there were two public houses, one post office, and a bus three times a week and twice on Saturdays.

Two years before there had been talk of the National Trust taking it over. When Brig and I arrived with our camping equipment to spend a week doing a survey on the valley's natural life it was at once apparent that things had changed. Large trucks, painted in a sickly yellow sped through the middle of the village at ten minute intervals. While we bought food at the post office and grocer's shop the lady behind the counter enthused about the progress that had been made since I was last in the village, 'You'll find things much different than when you were last here, what with the pits and the new houses, and young folk, there's a dance on Friday, in the church hall. You want to get yourselves there, plenty of people your own age. They have a marvellous time'. At least they still remembered you in the village, which was an encouraging sign.

I walked around the village, looking at the council houses they had built since I was last here, while Brig made a brass rubbing of the Latin inscription commemorating a local knight who had died in the second Crusade. An untidy woman was gathering in washing while two small children pulled at her skirts. The old age pensioners, sunning themselves on a bench under one of the green's large lime trees looked at me curiously. They were not used to seeing sixteen year old youths in shorts. Brig eventually finished the brass rubbing and came out of the church, talking to the vicar. The vicar, an elderly man, wished us well, sent his regards to farmer Butterfield and regretted that his car was broken down, otherwise he would have run us to our camp site. He cringed, as yet another of the heavy, yellow lorries trundled through the village, sending clouds of white dust over the old men seated on the bench.

The road out of the village curved upwards through a wooded lane. We had to follow this for a mile until we reached Mr. Butterfield's land. It was too hot to talk very much, although it was by now five in the afternoon. As we neared the crest of the hill a stream of motor-cycles, motor scooters and cars passed us, each loaded with dusty, tired looking workmen.

At the top of the hill we could see what the postmistress had meant by 'progress'. There were large mounds of soil. The river, which was normally clear, with long fronds of moving weeds and lazy chub, was coloured a bright yellow. Coarse weeds and nettles grew on the soil heaps and the fox gloves, for which I had remembered the river bank, were nowhere to be found. From craters in the ground the gaunt jibs of big dragline excavators poked up. About half a mile away was a large and clattering gravel washing plant. My companion became very indignant and spoke of vandals and modern planning which allowed the destruction of the countryside.

Picking our way along the river bank I saw that the soil heaps sprayed a fine yellow dust into the river. They were full of rabbit and rat holes, while docks and nettles were slowly embedding themselves into the banks. Four hundred yards up the river and away from the bridge we came to a levelled stretch of river bank. On it were two untidy huts, a large repair shop, and the gravel washing plant. Near the workshops some men were tipping sump oil on to a heap of dirty sacks, paper and old tyres. While we watched, a tall swarthy individual threw half a gallon of petrol on to the heap, stepped back and then threw a lighted taper. The rubbish quickly caught alight and the burning sent a thick column of smoke into the evening sky. The men nodded curtly to us, picked up their haversacks, climbed into a car and drove away.

Now the scene was deserted. A row of the lorries was parked alongside the gravel washer. Around the structure of conveyors and water sprays, were patches of sticky black mud and dark brown sand. I climbed up one of the elevators to get a look at the whole scene from above. Brig was idly kicking a small, discarded oil tin. The mining complex stretched down as far as the bridge, a quarter of a mile away, as well as upstream for a good half mile. At the far end was a small hut which housed a pumping station. Water was extracted from the river and came down a grey painted pipe line to the washing plant where I was now standing. Then, dirty and muddy, it was poured straight back into the river. Since we had first seen the site, the river had cleared, for gravel was no longer being washed and the sand had settled. But, although the water was clear, the river bed was heavily silted up with bright yellow sand. Water weed, unique as far as I knew to this river, now only appeared in small, frail patches.

I climbed down and Brig and myself ambled up the river bank, clambering over soil heaps. We lifted a heavy oil drum, which was dribbling oil slicks on to the water, and threw it into one of the craters where a dragline with a half ton bucket rested. We walked slowly up the valley to the farm.

18. Give an account of the life of a man or woman whom you admire. **[1 hour]**

Plan.

1. Blind.
2. Parent's attitude.
3. Early education.
4. Place in a special school.
5. New Principal.
6. Braille's determination to help the blind.
7. First alphabet.
8. Alphabet banned.
9. Perseverance.
10. Petitions to government. Braille's death.
11. Adoption of Braille's alphabet.

In the same year as Napoleon began his retreat from Moscow, a small French boy stabbed a knife into his left eye. His parents, saddlers and smallholders, distrusted doctors and allowed a local herbalist to treat the wound. She stemmed the outward bleeding but more seriously, the eye bled inwards. An infection contaminated the other eye and by the end of the year Louis Braille was blind. Later, he was to give the blind the best workable alphabet so far devised.

His parents and elder brothers were fortunately sensible and the child was encouraged to be as independent as possible. Highly gifted, Louis, by the age of six was producing marketable leather goods in his father's workshop. However, he became increasingly morose and lonely and many people thought he would never be able to support himself.

Fortunately, a philanthropist and priest, Abbé Jacques Palluy, undertook to educate the child privately. Taught first to identify bird songs Louis was soon proficient in music and could play several instruments. The priest also instilled a deep religious sense into the child which helped him to come to terms with his suffering and isolation. Under the guidance of his first teacher he progressed so well that he was able to attend the local school. He stayed for two years and gained a basic grounding in language and arithmetic. So impressed were the teachers with the child's dedication, alacrity and intelligence that they managed to get him sent to a special school, 'The National Institution for the Young Blind'.

For Louis this was a great opportunity. The institution was the only one in France. It had been started in 1783 by M. Hauy, a Junior Foreign Office Official who had been shocked at the way the blind were maltreated. Instead of gaining sympathy a blind person was a target for ridicule and cruel practical jokes. Often a blind child was sold by his parents to circuses or itinerant organ grinders. Begging was the usual means of gaining sustenance. Harsh discipline was enforced in the school, a dilapidated building in which slime and damp ran down the walls. Lessons were carried out by rote learning and the failure to understand was believed to stem from laziness and not from the handicap of blindness. Hence pupils were savagely beaten. Louis, separated from his family, was at first very lonely.

In 1819 a new Principal, Dr. Pignier, entered the College. He was more progressive than his predecessor and immediately took an interest in the talented pupil of the Institution. Under his guidance, Louis Braille learned mathematics, history, geography, and French grammar and won most of the school prizes. His musical talent, first shown in early childhood, developed.

In his early teens Louis summarised the problem imposed by blindness for himself and others. Speaking to his father he said,

> 'The blind are the loneliest people in the world. I can tell different birds by their song and I can find my way about with my stick, but without books the blind can never really learn'.

Alphabets did exist but these were made up of large embossed letters, often seven or eight inches high. As Louis knew from experience, the meaning of a sentence was often forgotten before the pupil had patiently transcribed the first few letters, a short book took up several volumes. Incisively intelligent, Louis realised that what was required was an alphabet formed with small letters. A French artillery officer who had used an embossed code of raised dots and dashes to pass messages at night gave Louis the inspiration for his alphabet.

His teenage years were spent trying to evolve an alphabet made up from embossed dots and dashes. At sixteen the first workable alphabet appeared. It was far from perfect, and Louis realised that his friends' and his own fingers were more susceptible to dots than dashes. With the luck that often accompanies genius and hard work the lay out of dominoes was followed. Variations were worked around six large and small dots. In 1834 the Braille alphabet was completed. Sixty three combinations to cover the letters of the alphabet, digits, and common words were worked out.

Success was not to follow. No one outside the Institution was interested, whilst inside the building the governors and some teachers were suspicious of their talented pupil. Supported, however, by Dr. Pignier, Braille went on to write a musical alphabet. He was appointed as a teacher. Each Sunday he visited, in turn, three parish churches, to play the organ for a small sum of money. Finally, not only was his alphabet not adopted, but his patron, Dr. Pignier, was dismissed because he had allowed a text book to be transcribed in Braille.

Dr. Dufau, Pignier's successor, was contemptuous of Louis and forbade the use of his alphabet. In despair, Louis took to teaching his methods clandestinely and his perseverance eventually won, for the alphabet eventually crept back into use. Enlightened teachers and blind pupils realised its merits even if those in authority did not.

In 1851 two petitions were presented to the French parliament, the first to adopt the Braille alphabet, the second to award Louis a Legion of Honour. Both petitions failed and by this time Louis was seriously ill. Years spent in the dank Institution building had led to a breakdown in his health. He had first contracted tuberculosis at twenty six. By 1851 he was seriously ill. In 1852 he died and was buried in Coupvray, his native village.

A Dr. Armitage lost his sight in 1868. An educated man, he devoted his work to analysing the various touch reading alphabets which had recently appeared and which had caused chaos in schools for the blind. A pupil taught in Manchester to read by touch would not understand the system used in Bristol. After two years work Braille's alphabet was declared to be superior to all the others. The 'English Braille Printing and Publishing House' was set up. Later it was to become 'The Royal Institute for the Blind'. Obscure and modest in his own lifetime, Braille's name has since become a household word. Its originator never sought fame, and desired only to help and inspire those afflicted like himself. However, in 1952, the country which had refused him a Legion of Honour a century before removed his remains from the modest French churchyard to the Parthenon of Paris, the resting place of all France's great warriors, statesmen and scholars.

19. A famous cathedral. **[1 hour]**

Plan.

1. Ely Cathedral in the Fens.
2. First religious foundation.
3. A centre for pilgrims in Middle Ages.
4. Developments to the 11th century.
5. Twelfth century developments.
6. Alterations due because of collapse of part of structure.
7. Building of the Lady Chapel.
8. Changing function of the cathedral.
9. Victorian alterations.

Ely Cathedral can be favourably compared with the great cathedrals of Britain and Europe. It towers out of the flat East Anglian Fens, to dominate the small market town and the surrounding countryside. Local people say that on a clear day it can be seen from twenty five or thirty miles away. Its history is long and chequered.

The first religious foundation was made at Ely when only coot, hern and duck lived with any comfort in the area. The land on which the first buildings appeared was a small island surrounded by estuarine marshes. That any religious building appeared in Ely is due solely to St. Etheldreda. Twice married, Etheldreda eventually gained her wish to found a religious community. She came to Ely, which was part of her dowry gift to her husband and founded a nunnery. In 673 A.D. the Archbishop of York installed her as Abbess of the community. Six years later she died of plague.

With a thriving cult of relics in the Middle Ages, Etheldreda's tomb, moved after her death inside the Church, made Ely a centre for many pilgrims. Nothing of the far off days of nearly thirteen hundred years ago remains, except for the stone base of a cross, standing in the south nave aisle bearing the words 'Lucem tuam ovino da deus et requiem. Amen'. This cross commemorates Ovin, an Anglian nobleman who came to Ely to help Etheldreda with her new foundation.

So great were the associations of piety and sanctity with Ely itself, that Danish pillage and war did not stop a community from returning there after the monastery was sacked in about 870. King Edgar revived the community and it became a Benedictine foundation until the Reformation. A new church, again destined to be destroyed was ordained in 970. Hereward the Wake, the only effective soldier to challenge the Norman Conquest after the death of King Harold, used the cathedral and monastery as a base for his guerrilla army. When the inevitable end came however, William allowed the religious community to continue but a Norman monk was given control and the building that one sees today began to grow from his efforts.

By about 1100 the eastern end of the Church looked much as it does now. The building was eventually completed in 1189 although several additions were later made. The Gallilee porch was constructed on the Western side of the building to accommodate the numerous pilgrims who came to venerate the various tombs. Hugh de Northwold destroyed the eastern apse of the cathedral and erected early English presbytery bays, and St. Etheldreda's tomb was finally transferred there.

The third alteration added originality to the design of the Cathedral. In 1322 the tower which stood in the centre of the building collapsed. Luckily, the energetic Alan of Walsingham was there to take charge. In conjunction with Edward III's carpenter, William Hurley, he decided to open out the space and leave room for a choir. To fill the area left by the tower it was decided to build a medieval lantern, weighing four hundred tons and which had to be supported from the walls of the octagon. How this was achieved by men with little more to hand than ropes, pulleys and timber scaffold is a mystery. However, the result, a high vaulted dome, giving way to a high octagon with inlet windows, is unique. Standing under it, it is interesting to speculate how long modern engineers would take to achieve the same effect.

The last feature of the Cathedral to be built was directed by a Monk, John of Wisbech. His task was to build a new lady chapel on the North Side of the Presbytery and to connect it with the Cathedral by a covered aisle. The interior of this building must have been spectacular, for it was painted in bright colours while statues told the life story of Etheldreda. Regrettably, the statues did not survive the extreme Puritanism of the fens, and an iconoclast smashed them with hammers and chisels. Another change to the Lady Chapel has come about from the whitening of the walls. When built the aspect of the Chapel would have been one of dark glowing lights.

Despite the Reformation, a monastic community remained at Ely under a new foundation made by Henry VIII, for it was unique for a monastery to be associated with a Cathedral. Some damage, such as the smashing of the shrines of the founding Saints took place, but the original choir stalls, built to Alan of Walsingham's direction still remain. Buildings around the Cathedral itself suffered most. Various structures were put to new uses. The old infirmary, its chapel and the Priory still remained however, and are incorporated in the King's School. The last man to cause any destruction in Ely was Oliver Cromwell who objected to the frequent singing and the lack of preaching. All the cloisters disappeared

Damage was not to cease however for some alterations to the interior layout were made in the eighteenth century. These spoiled the symmetry and grand design of the building.

Fortunately for the Cathedral and present day worshippers and visitors, a vigorous Dean, Dr. Peacock, arrived in 1839. He did away with 'improvements' of the previous century, restored the old plan, and saw that the structural fabric was repaired before it was irrepairably damaged. So great was the success achieved by this man—he also revised the services—that Mr. Gladstone spoke of Ely as 'a pattern for the Cathedrals of England'.

20. Which country would you like to visit? Give reasons for your choice. [1 hour]

Plan.

1. Islands which make up Japan.
2. Tourist attractions.
3. Modern urban Japan.
4. Developments of industry and technology.
5. Shipbuilding, engineering, electronics.
6. Old culture.

Four large islands—Honshu, Shikoku, Kyushu, and Hokkaido—make up the major land mass of Japan. Stretching 1,500 miles down the North Eastern Pacific, Japan is one and a half times larger than Britain. For the holiday maker the island chain is ideal.

85% of the land is mountainous. Mt. Fuji soars 12,375 feet into the sky while many other peaks exceed 5,000 feet. With this terrain Japan is spectacularly beautiful, for the mountains are enhanced by numerous lakes, volcanoes and hot springs. Well designed holiday sites have been laid out around the springs and there are adequate facilities for the tourist, for the Japanese have found that foreign visitors are a valuable source of revenue. Besides the traditional mountaineering and skiing there is the attractive coastline. Fiords and small islands are frequent and again these make ideal holiday sites. Small fishing villages, still living the traditional life of a hundred years ago can be found. However, alongside these remote villages are modern ports with their myriad attractions. So for scenery and recreational facilities Japan has much to offer.

Much more than a visitor's idyll, Japan is a modern nation with lessons to teach the Europeans and Americans. As 85% of the nation's land is mountainous, 95 million people have to live in an area about the size of Wales and land pressure has made Tokio the world's largest city with more than 9 million people. While thousands still live in shanty towns, the majority live in large blocks of flats. Comprehensive rail services make the rush hour no worse than that in London. For one interested in the future of urban development, Japan demonstrates, in manifold ways, the pitfalls and successes of town planning.

In most spheres of modern industry Japan can match and sometimes exceed the west. Agriculture is highly specialised and rice growing technology is the best in the world. Paddy fields run to the base and up the lower slopes of the mountains in a series of intensely cultivated terraces. Nagasaki's shipyards demonstrates the latest techniques in large scale shipbuilding and the tankers produced there are amongst the largest in the world.

Little need be said of Japan's prowess in the manufacture of motorcycles, motor vehicles and electrical equipment. Japan's success in the Isle of Man's T.T. motor cycle races appears annually in the newspapers. Again transistor radios and transistorised television sets have appeared on the Western markets. A country experiencing success of this kind would be tantalising to a visitor.

The old Japan still exists beside the new, industrial Japan. Only in 1868 was the nation effectively opened to the West. Within a hundred years the traditions of centuries have been broken and yet have remained. In the western world the values of pre-industrial civilisation vanished with the industrial revolution. Folk art in the west is largely dead. In Japan this is not so, for the traditional ritualistic ceremonies, and the highly ordered ancient social life continues. Geisha girls and the mandarin culture co-exist with high powered industry and urban complexes. People who lament at the visible passing of older values could take a profitable look at Japan and see how she has preserved the old with the new.

21. Write an article suitable for a magazine describing the attractions for the holidaymaker of one of the following—a small seaside town. a small village, a small holiday camp. [30 min.]

Plan.

1. Introduction—brief history—description.
2. Scenic beauty—activity—old town.
3. New town.
4. Fishing.
5. Countryside.
6. Assessment.

Whitby is an ancient fishing port built at the mouth of the River Esk in Yorkshire. For centuries small trawlers and drifters have sailed from the river anchorage to catch cod and herring in the North Sea. On the south cliff above the town there is an abbey where the Venerable Bede once lived.

The town has grown on both sides of the river. The old part, on the south side, is picturesque with its houses built in local Yorkshire stone and roofed with bright red pan tiles. There is always something going on in the harbour, and the fishermen welcome holidaymakers. If you decided to go there in August, the continental fishing fleets, chasing the herring, will be using the harbour, and there will be many different nationalities in the port—Russians, Poles, Norwegians, Dutch, French and Belgians.

There are many very good small hotels and boarding houses in the new part of the town. Also, there are caravan sites and chalets which can be hired for a week or a fortnight. For young people there are numerous camping grounds with modern facilities. The shops are well stocked and the town excels itself in the manufacture of handmade goods—woven baskets, locally produced pottery and glass, and numerous worthwhile souvenirs.

Fishing is a popular pastime, both from the pier at the harbour entrance and from the jetty. Beginners and old hands are welcome and local fishermen are always willing to take out parties. One old salt who sells fishing tackle goes down to the quay side or on to the pier to supervise his youthful novice customers. He will even supply bait free of charge and his yarns about shipwrecks and smuggling have been retold all over England.

Perhaps Whitby is not the best town to choose for young people who want rowdy dance halls, but for the family with small children, or for people who have grown up families and want a peaceful holiday, Whitby is very good value.

22. Write a character sketch of your doctor or dentist. [30 min.]

Plan.

1. Introduction—name and appearance of dentist.
2. Trust and confidence he inspired.
3. Cheerful—efficient.
4. Persônality—seen in his conversation.
5. Anger at the inefficiency of others.
6. Personal feelings—details.

My dentist is called Mr. Uboe. He is a young man from Malawi who is completing his training as a dental surgeon at N . . . . Infirmary. He is six feet tall, has black short hair and wears tortoise shell spectacles. He is always immaculate in his white starched overalls.

I used to be frightened to go to the dentist. My previous dentist was a foxy looking man called Mr. Donks, who never had any patience. I never trusted him after he smashed a tooth to bits with his forceps and pulled it out in about six pieces. The gum became infected and I decided to find another dentist.

Mr. Uboe, unlike Mr. Donks, is cheerful and puts his patients at ease. He tells me what he has to do, and if it is going to hurt, he warns me to be ready for it. Yet, he rarely hurts me. His hands are very steady and he concentrates extremely hard when he is drilling teeth. Also, as soon as he is near a nerve he stops drilling for a moment or two.

Unlike most dentists he talks a good deal. He has told me all about the school he went to in Africa and about his first impressions of England. Although he has had to work at a very hard course for five years and is still training he never lets this worry him. He asks me a lot of questions about the school I am going to and is very interested because I want to be an electrical engineer. This may be because he has a younger brother who wants to be a civil engineer.

The only time that he becomes angry is when a filling works loose. My teeth are peculiar in this, and he has to be very painstaking to make the fillings set properly. However, he does not blame me, but the manufacturers for making poor filling material. Occasionally, he says he thinks he will go to America to study further because he feels the science of dentistry is not yet well enough developed.

At other times he seems to be homesick and talks a great deal about his father and mother. He also tells me that people overseas suffer a great deal because there are not enough doctors and dentists to treat them. When he talks like this I feel guilty because he is having to spend time treating me when other dentists, even Mr. Donks, are available in Britain.

23. Explain to a foreigner the main duties of the English police force. [30 min.]

Plan.

1. Prevention and detection of crime.
2. Development of methods to cope with the modern criminal.
3. C.I.D.
4. Traffic control.
5. Respect for the police.

The main duty of the English police force is the prevention and detection of crime. In recent years spectacular crimes, like the Great Train Robbery have captured popular imagination. Many people in Britain and elsewhere imagine the police force tackling villainous master criminals everyday. However, such crimes are comparatively rare and the real job of the police is much less glamorous than newspaper reports and modern films would have us believe. Crime is increasing in Britain and it has trebled since 1938. Money and expensive personal items are usually the target of the burglar. A routine enquiry into the thefts of a fur coat or transistor radio can take many hours.

The modern criminal uses up-to-date equipment and usually has the element of surprise on his side. To cope with this the police have developed a vast administrative organisation and evolved an international network—Interpol. Once the local 'bobby' patrolled his beat on foot; now, a panda car with two-way radio covers his 'patch' more efficiently. Convicted criminals are photographed for inclusion in a rogues' gallery. Detailed records and photographs are kept on microfilm. Some police force members spend their working lives in laboratories, identifying fingerprints and checking for blood stains and all the minute clues unwittingly left.

The particularly serious crimes are handled by the specialist branch of the police force, the C.I.D. These men rarely wear uniforms. Indeed, they often adopt different guises to gain inside information. Sometimes a burglar is caught because the police recognise the method he used to break into a house. Trained to detect signs which an ordinary person would miss, they can often gauge, for example, by the way in which a door has been forced, who might have been responsible. Within the police force there are specialist branches dealing with smuggling, the control of narcotics and with fraud.

The motor car driver forms the largest sector of the public to come in contact with the police. Traffic control and the implementation of traffic legislation take up much police time. Vehicles, large and small, have to be guided through the towns of Britain because road building has not kept abreast of the number of vehicles on the roads. Parking offences figure prominently in English courts, and again it is the police constables' job (aided today by the ubiquitous traffic warden) to report offenders.

English police are respected by the public. They are always present where large crowds congregate—at football matches, in busy shopping centres and at dance halls. The very presence of the blue uniform has a calming effect.

24. Describe a local character whom you find interesting.
[30 min.]

Plan.

1. Origins of Tom.
2. Appearance.
3. Knowledgeable.
4. A happy man.

Tom came from Norfolk originally. In 1910, aged nine, he tramped northwards with a gang of unemployed farm workers. They eventually found work in North Yorkshire. He returned to his home county the following spring but by 1912 he was back. Except for a few short holidays he has lived in the north all his life. When asked why he swapped the picturesque scenery of North Norfolk for the undulating countryside of the Tees Valley he only blinks and says, 'There were too many small farmers down there, so there were no jobs so I left'.

Superficially he looks like the traditional English rustic. He wears overalls, Wellington boots, a sports jacket and a leather sleeveless jerkin. In winter, when the weather is wet or cold, he puts on an old home guard coat, reaching nearly to his ankles. A cap adds the final touch to his dress. He rarely drinks, occasionally smokes a pipe and frequently chews tobacco and his teeth are stained a deep brown from this habit.

His appearance belies his true nature. In his seventies he remains a skilled farm worker. As a boy he learned to plough with horses and perfected all the now dead farm crafts such as ditching, hedge laying, and stack thatching. Unlike many land workers of his generation he quickly grew accustomed to the tractors and sophisticated machinery that were first introduced into the area in the 1930's. He never hankered after the 'old days' : instead he learned to use the new tools and became as great an expert with combine harvesters and caterpillar tractors as he had been with horses. A life out of doors has kept him remarkably healthy. His face, wind beaten over the years, gives him a deceptively young looking appearance. He still works eight hours a day as the foreman of a large farm. His employer would let him retire at any time but in Tom's shrewd old mind he knows that 'folks who pack up go to bed and then they die'.

On nature he is a mine of information. He knows the habits of most animals and birds and is quick to spot a rare species. One day he discovered a large ungainly bird stranded in a kale field and immediately knew it was a rare great northern diver. Tom carried the bird to the river where it happily took off and continued its long migratory journey south.

Tom has a patient mature outlook that few possess. This has been shaped by working the land and tending stock He has a gentle pride in raising the best crops in the district for over fifty years. Certainly he seems to be that rare species, a happy man.

25. What are the problems of transport in your home district? [1 hour]

Plan.

1. Introduce location.
2. Railway closures.
3. Nature of roads—arises because of terrain.
4. Difficulty of building a modern road—purposeless.
5. Local knowledge—adequate for local people—visitors should walk.
6. No serious local problem—only a problem for car driving tourists—but part of a National Park—Yorkshire wants hikers not drivers.
7. Conclusion.

Transport problems exist for other people in my home district. I live high on the Yorkshire Pennines in a remote cottage with my parents. Many people say we are isolated and shut off but we like it that way. There are problems for some but this is part of the price one pays for solitude and untrammelled countryside.

Until the Beeching plan was introduced the railway line to Leyburn and Hawes was the only simple way of moving large quantities of goods quickly and easily. Minerals used to be carried from the hills to the Teeside industrial areas and in return coal used to be brought in by rail. Now that the railways have gone, the roads are the only means of transport for goods and individuals.

Roads through the Yorkshire Dales twist and snake. They follow the paths and contours of the hills that men had to follow when they guided mule trains down the hills with panniers of lead on their backs two hundred years ago. And the roads the leadminers took were the same roads that medieval merchants followed. The unchanging routes are not due to whim or tradition; they are the only practicable ones.

A modern dual carriageway could be built through the Yorkshire Dales. Thousands of tons of rock and peat would have to be blasted and all the best farmland in the valley bottoms would disappear. The cost would be prohibitive, and would not be of much use either,for there are already major roads across the Pennines further south in the West Riding.

Local drivers and livestock carriers who know the roads manage quite well round the sharp bends and steep cambers. Holidaymakers, who come to see the Yorkshire Dales in their motor cars, are the people who are vexed at our backwardness. They creep up Swaledale and Arkengarthdale, seeing little of the hills because of the concentration needed to stop them plunging into ravines. They will never know the Dales properly because they will not walk. Footpaths are still the best ways of seeing the hills. Picnicking on a piece of tarmac, laid on the roadside by the benevolent North Riding County Council is feeble compared with the sights to be seen should people walk perhaps a mile or half mile higher up the hill.

Perhaps, at some far off date, helicopters will be introduced to ferry visitors in. Dalesmen would not approve. However, after the first few crashes, due to the air currents blowing down the Pennine gaps the venture will undoubtedly be dropped. Little change that is worthwhile can be made. People who live in the Dales can manage, and if they can cope, there is no reason why the hillsides should be gouged and mauled to let volumes of summer time traffic through.

The problems are slight, provided people are sensible. There is no need to bring a car up the Dales. People would be better off walking and camping.

26. A famous inventor. **[1 hour]**

Plan.

1. Background.
2. First job.
3. Marriage.
4. Work on railways and mines.
5. 'Blucher'. Pit lamp.
6. Darlington to Stockton line.
7. Views on railway engineering.
8. Factory.
9. Manchester to Liverpool line.
10. Chat Moss.
11. 'The Rocket'.
12. Fame in later life.

Fate seemed against George Stephenson ever becoming more than an obscure collier. He narrowly avoided becoming a farm worker. His first job was to watch cows and check them from straying. His wage was twopence a day. With his brothers and sisters he lived in a dilapidated cottage and never went to school. The one thing in his favour was that he lived near a coal field and that was where the first railed-ways were being built. Horses drew tubs along wooden rails.

When at twelve he decided he did not like a farm man's job his father, a pumpman in a local mine, got him a job at sixpence a day picking pieces of shale out of the coal. The work was back breaking but the youth persisted, hoping for better work later. After a few months he was promoted to driving a horsedrawn coal tub and at fourteen was one of the pumping engine mechanics. He eventually went to work at one of the Duke of Northumberland's collieries. Soon he took charge of an engine and was then given the responsible job of watching the water levels and checking that the pump was still drawing water. Already he had ideas of becoming an engineer, of following in the footsteps of Watt who had succeeded from a similar background.

His first schooling cost him one penny an hour with a local schoolteacher who taught him English. At eighteen he was learning what a six year old boy knew. Once he had mastered elementary English he started to study Mathematics, paying two pence an hour. More promotion in the pit followed, and at twenty he was a brakesman with charge over the winding gear which pulled men and coal up from the face. At this time he proposed to a rich farmer's daughter but was turned down as being socially unsuitable.

Shortly after his twenty first birthday he married the daughter of a lesser farmer. He rented a labourer's cottage and a year later his son was born. Robert was three when his mother died. George's reputation was beginning to spread by this time. He went to Montrose to look at an engine which was giving trouble, leaving his son in the charge of his easy going neighbours. He put the faulty engine right after most of the notable engineers had failed and returned home, twenty eight pounds better off to find that misfortune was overtaking him. His father had been blinded by a steam jet and would never be able to work again. No industrial benefits were available. Stephenson had to support his father and son and find the money needed to buy himself out of compulsory military service which he considered would be a waste of time for him. Probably if he could have afforded the fare he would have sailed for America.

His savings, amounting to £100, were put towards Robert's education. Astride a donkey, the boy travelled each day to a school in Newcastle. Soon the child was to prove his ability. Meanwhile his father was substituting winding gear for horses and was successfully drawing heavier loads out of the mine shafts and up and down the colliery slopes. Several locomotives had already been built. One had blown up. another had crashed. Trevithic, the Cornish engineer, had he had the patience, could have perfected a locomotive. The astute Stephenson saw his chance and managed to persuade the colliery owner, Lord Ravensworth, to give the plan his blessing.

His first engine he named 'Blucher' in honour of the famous Prussian general who had helped defeat Napoleon. Installed at Killingworth pit, this engine would pull eight wagons weighing more than thirty tons. Lord Ravensworth was delighted but Stephenson saw this as only the beginning. At the same time he found time to invent a mechanical scarecrow, a self rocking cradle and an alarm clock for rousing the colliery workers. He invented a miners' safety lamp also. A bitter controversy arose, because the eminent chemist, Sir Humphry Davy, succeeded at the same time (1815) and many said the self educated northerner had merely copied Davy's design. The outcome was that Davy received a prize of £2,000 whereas Stephenson had to be content with the runner's up prize of £100.

Although depressed he began work on his third engine and was then asked to construct a railed way from Hetton Colliery to the River Wear. This was the first enterprise in which father and son worked together. He finally married Elizabeth Hindmarsh, whose father had once thought his daughter was socially superior to Stephenson. Having made his name, Stephenson was seen as an admirable match.

The achievement which was to make Stephenson famous was the building of the Darlington to Stockton railway line. The engineer heard that Edward Pease, a colliery owner, was proposing to build a mineral line between Darlington and Stockton. Wooden rails were to be used and horses were to draw the wagons. Stephenson approached Pease to build a railway. He had to do two things; to persuade Pease that he could himself build the line and that a projected canal should not be built.

Stephenson's astute reasoning can be seen in a pamphlet preserved in Darlington library. He argued that canals took longer to build and were more expensive to maintain than railways. He pointed out that drought and frost could impede them in summer and winter. As construction time for a canal took longer, the interest on capital loans would be necessarily greater. Finally, railways were the future means of transport. Pease was won over to the local engineer's arguments and the railway was built to Stephenson's specifications.

A factory for building locomotives was opened. Robert was placed in charge of this, while George went off to survey the track. Much local opposition was encountered from farmers and road owners and on 27 September 1825 a large crowd gathered, hopeful of chaos, explosion and disaster. However, 'the signal being given the engine started off with (its) . . . immense train of carriages: and such was its velocity that in some parts the speed was frequently twelve miles an hour'. By the time Stephenson, driving the engine, had reached Stockton over six hundred people had scrambled on board. Soon a successful service was established.

Ahead lay much bigger tasks for the engineering team of George and Robert. They were invited to build a railway from Manchester to Liverpool. Opposition came both from landowners and canal operators, who, correctly, saw their livelihood ruined. Farmers said fumes would ruin their crops and frighten animals, whilst aristocratic landowners feared for nesting birds and their game reserves. Stephenson had to spend much time avoiding gamekeepers and farm men who would have ducked him; often he made his surveys by moonlight. A special bill had to go before Parliament and when Stephenson appeared there Barristers, unused to his northern accent, teased and baited him. He was generally confused by the deliberately complicated questions but, in a modified form, the bill was passed and the line went ahead.

One of the biggest tasks was the crossing of Chat Moss, a dismal marsh. It would not bear the weight of a man let alone a steam engine. It was decided to build a raised track, supported on timber and clinker, and this Stephenson supervised. Workmen had to fix planks of wood to their feet to cross the quagmire. To the surprise of all except Stephenson and a few enthusiasts the venture succeeded.

The line built, a competition took place for the best engine. There were five contestants but Stephenson's engine, 'The Rocket', won. All the dignitaries of the country including the Duke of Wellington and Peel were there. Fanny Kemble, the noted actress described Stephenson as follows:

> 'His face is fine, though careworn, and bears an expression of deep thoughtfulness: his mode of explaining his ideas is peculiar and very original, striking and forcible. . . . He has certainly turned my head'.

The event was marred by one thing: the death of Huskisson, who was knocked over by one of the locomotives and died in a nearby manor house.

Railway construction continued rapidly and by 1846 London was linked with most of the provincial cities. After being considered a madman and crank by many and an imposter by others Stephenson was suddenly famous. Twice he was obliged to refuse a knighthood. He sat on select committees in the House of Commons. He travelled to Spain and Belgium as a technical adviser.

Stephenson and his son became very rich and George bought Tapton House near Chesterfield. However, he also remembered the people he had been brought up with and helped where he could. For his workers he introduced a compensation and superannuation scheme. He died in 1848, leaving a personal fortune of £140,000. Robert, who had always been delicate, only lived another eleven years, but in that time had raised the family fortune to more than £400,000. On his death a monument to father and son was raised in Westminster Abbey.

27. Write about any film you have seen which impressed you. [1 hour]

Plan.

1. Importance of electrical power.
2. Special problems of building Kariba Dam.
3. Initial surveys.
4. Construction of feeder roads and transport of equipment.
5. Method of construction of main dam.
6. Levelling of forests. Movement of people.
7. Rescue of wildlife.
8. Power stations.
9. Expertise of film-makers.

What steam was to the first industrial revolution, electrical power is to present day industrial developments. All over the world electrical power is emerging as the dominant power in the home and in industry. Few industries today could exist without it, many homes would be lost without it. Advanced countries develop new power plants at immense cost and developing countries see electrical power as the dynamic factor in their race to mass production and the resultant higher standards of living.

A film on the construction of the Kariba dam showed the multiple facets of exploiting the electrical resources of an emerging country. To bridge the Zambesi river, running between Rhodesia and Zambia, and to use the water to generate hydro-electrical power, was to stem the mightiest river in Africa. As the commentator on the film's soundtrack pointed out, the task was not a project but a campaign.

After geological and hydrographic surveys had been taken a decision was reached to dam the river across the Kariba gorge. Set in inaccessible terrain, roads had to be built to allow the convoys of equipment and fuel supplies to reach the site. Bunkering facilities for the fourteen million gallons of fuel oil needed had to be erected. Plants had to be designed to supply three hundred and fifty thousand tons of concrete that the construction would eventually consume. Servicing facilities had to be provided for the ten thousand men of all nationalities engaged on the project. All this work was ancillary to the main task—bridging the Zambesi.

Before work could commence on the dam itself, diversion tunnels for the river had to be built. With the river's flow reduced to a minimum across the proposed site of the dam, coffer dams were erected. These were massive constructions which encircled an area of the river bed holding back the water, while the engineers and construction men worked twenty four hours a day to construct the main dam. Eventually the first coffer dam was detonated and water allowed to surge through the partly constructed dam.

Having diverted the river a second time, a further coffer dam had to be built to allow the men to work on the central section of the main dam. Patiently the engineers inched their way across the river. Local tribesmen had been sceptical as to the success of the scheme. They reasoned that their God would be angry and that he would arouse the river, in the wet season, to sweep away the work of the foreign engineers. They were almost right. Floods, thought only to occur once every ten thousand years, did sweep part of the dam away and delayed work for six months. The film showed men risking their lives to secure equipment and beat the waters threatening to wreck their work. Engineering skill and courage eventually prevailed, but the filming of the flood was a salutary warning that when man interferes with nature he should be prepared to fight her in all her strength and power.

The film gave the impression that the planners had catered for all that could be foreseen. Twinned bulldozers, dragging large balls and chains tore down acre upon acre of trees. This was carried out so that the future fishing industry that the dam would create would not be hampered by nets snarling on submerged timber. A further sequence in the film showed tribal leaders explaining to their people that they would have to move from their traditional villages. For the lake that the Kariba dam would cause would be one hundred and seventy miles long. Perhaps in an age of technology these peoples were the real sufferers. However, the film was at pains to point out that the life that awaited the tribes in new areas would be materially better than the life they had formerly lived. Despite this emphasis on the 'better' life ahead for the displaced peoples involved, one had the impression that the film makers were using overt propaganda. On this point only time will tell.

Creating what amounted to an inland sea, endangered the life of countless wild animals and land reptiles such as snakes, scorpions and tortoises, all part of nature's delicate balance. The wildlife trust did mount an operation to save marooned animals from drowning. That people could find time to do this was impressive, as were some of the rescues made. A particularly stark sequence was the towing to shore of a five ton female elephant. In this case the rescuers in 'Operation Noah' succeeded. However, with all the good intentions in the world, countless animals must have perished as they retreated before the flood to higher land and eventually to the trees. But the film-makers did have the honesty to show the rescue of animals and for this they deserve praise.

The latter sequences of the film showed the construction completed and the river checked. Electrical generators were installed, turbines capable of producing three hundred thousand volts of electricity. Building the power station and the grid lines, carrying the new wealth over three hundred miles to the coal and copper fields, was in itself a massive task. Despite reservations over the displaced tribes and the drowned animals the overall impression was one of a brilliant feat of engineering which would bring ultimate good to the peoples involved.

Finally, one must praise the skill of the film makers. Shooting in colour they brought out the richness and variety of the countryside extremely well and their enthusiasm was communicated to the viewer. Care over details was taken. The soundtrack was especially composed and this incorporated a tantalising background to the visual effects. In short, the film was most worthwhile. It stands the acid test from the viewer's standpoint, it is worth seeing a second time.

28. Describe a scene you will never forget. [1¼ hours]

Plan.

1. Set the scene.
2. First hint of activity.
3. Invitation.
4. The shoot.
5. Excitement.
6. Scene of death.

A light covering of snow lay on the ground. The sky was sporadically cloudy, with a yellow sun breaking through in places. Sycamores, chestnuts, ashes and elms stood, stark and bare in the large wood to my right. Further away, at a distance of about a mile, was a plantation of sombre green fir trees. The hills behind the plantation were snow-capped and dotted with dark coniferous trees. I continued my walk towards the wood, picking my way across the rutted, frozen field.

As I neared the wood, which I knew bordered the River Tees, I saw several vehicles parked. Five landrovers, two shooting brakes, and an open truck with their owners standing around them appeared strange on a Boxing Day morning. At random intervals sticks were stuck in the ground with numbers on them. I walked on, wondering what they were all doing at this time of day.

When I was two hundred yards away I saw that they were carrying guns. I stopped and waited. They saw me and waved me on, so obediently I walked forward. The party was cheerful, asked me if I was enjoying my walk, then an aged militaristic gentleman saw my camera and said, 'Bet he can't stop one in flight'. One what?' 'Don't you know what we are? We're shooting game. A party of men will be walking through that wood soon, and we shoot anything that comes out. You'll get some good photographs if you stay'. I said 'Thank you' and stood well back.

I made several adjustments to my camera and looked up as a fat pheasant flew overhead flapping its wings loudly. Two men shot at it but missed. As I had been adjusting my camera, the party, nine in all, had walked out to the separate sticks, and stood, waiting patiently for their sport. Everyone had romping labradors or slobbering spaniels—gun dogs chosen for their retrieving rather than their personal appeal. Three pheasants came out together and I had one sighted through the range finder on my camera when it stopped, spun, a cloud of feathers spattering from its flesh, and spiralled to earth. A second later two more pheasants fell earthwards. One, trailing a wing tried to run lopsided back to the wood.

but a big black labrador chased it, caught it and carried the wounded, squawking bird back to its owner. He promptly wrang its neck, and waited for more birds to appear. In increasing numbers the birds left their fir tree sanctuary. All had to fly over the line of strategically placed guns. Some made exceptionally lucky flights; one was shot at eleven times yet was still unharmed. Most were less fortunate. There would be a bang, the sound of wind blowing through the bird's feathers as it dropped earthwards and then a 'thump' as it hit the ground. I saw through the range finder on the camera several pheasants hit in flight.

Suddenly, I was caught up in the excitement, pushing the handle on my camera time after time. It became a game with me, as to whether I could capture a pheasant in flight with my new telephoto lens, before one of the shooting party hit it. I hoped to get just one picture of a pheasant at the instant when pellets ripped into its flesh and membranes. Then it was over. A line of men advanced from the wood, and tapped the last of the undergrowth with their sticks. They climbed the fence, whilst a man in plus fours—undoubtedly the gamekeeper—shouted instructions to them.

I looked around me. Dead game birds, cock and hen pheasants, a woodcock, two guinea fowl and a hare were dead within ten yards of me. A large cock pheasant lay dying, a tear of blood forming in one staring eye. As I removed the telephoto lenses to take a picture of it. it died, its eye weakly closing as I watched. Dead and dying birds, beautifully mottled and speckled were pushed into game bags while the sportsmen congratulated themselves on their shooting. One had to admire their skill: I knew how hard it was to hit a bird in flight with the camera: it would be equally hard to hit it with a cartridge. So many defenceless, graceful birds had died to demonstrate this skill.

The party gathered up its equipment, climbed into its various cars and drove away. A pheasant flew back into the wood and all was quiet once more.

29. Describe a character whom you dislike and can never forget. [45 min.]

Plan.

1. Mr. Beaver.
2. Myself and history and cricket.
3. Humiliation at cricket practice.
4. Dislike.
5. Further humiliation.
6. Later.

Mr. Beaver was the only schoolmaster I actively disliked. Some of the masters were dull, others gave severe punishments, but Mr. Beaver was different. Thin, aquiline and immensely fit he was hostile to anyone who was weak at cricket. He equated weakness at this sport with inferiority. His subject was history. Many years of teaching had taught him to expect little from boys aged between eleven and fifteen. His lessons were informal and largely devoted to drawing maps of numerous battle campaigns. He had little time for anyone who read history on their own. In his athletic mind, private reading was unhealthy and unnatural. I would have been all right if I had been weak at history. For, being a very mediocre cricketer and poor historian I would have fitted in with Beaver's scheme of things. Regrettably I liked history.

Usually I was near the top of the set at school. I drew the maps of the Napoleonic wars and the First World War. I read about them. All seemed to be fine, until one day, in the summer term of the second year, Mr. Beaver put me on his 'rising talent' cricket list. Padded, and with bat in hand I reluctantly made my way to the cricket nets. I shuddered when I saw three of the fastest bowlers in the school limbering up.

In three overs, accompanied by a caustic commentary from Mr. Beaver I skied eleven catches, was bowled seven times and knocked my stumps down once. Mr. Beaver refused to believe this, and so there were another three overs in which I was cleaned bowled eight times and gave several more easy catches. Finally Mr. Beaver told me to leave the stumps down and concentrate on hitting the ball. But I could not manage this and finally, humiliated, I slunk back to the changing rooms. I decided I would go back to house leagues cricket, organised by the school scripture teacher and vicar. This was my level; a league designed for those without cricketing ability.

I was welcomed back and celebrated by dropping four catches and hitting twenty three runs. But from then on there was to be no peace from Mr. Beaver. He made sarcastic remarks about my history work. I dropped from third to nineteenth position in the class. I was included in every punishment, whether it be learning lines, writing them or going for compulsory cross country runs. In one summer term I wrote three thousand two hundred lines and ran seven marathons of five and a half miles.

No rapprochement existed in Mr. Beaver's mind between my total lack of interest in cricket and my intelligence and ability with history. In the third form I finally rebelled after a particularly unpleasant hour and a half. By way of entertainment Mr. Beaver had decided to demonstrate how a Roman centurion used his spear. I was told 'be a Teutonic barbarian, here's your shield' and I was presented with the classroom fireguard. Mr. Beaver pranced and danced and jabbed at me while I fended him off as best I could. He won of course, and I returned to my desk, suffering from numerous bruises and winded from a jab in the stomach.

The rest of the class loved it. I walked out. I went to the library and said that I was not going to his history lessons. Amazingly I got away with it. Perhaps no one knew where I was for the next two terms. Perhaps Mr. Beaver had refused to have me back. Anyway, I spent my time browsing through numerous books and reading what interested me. I did not draw any more history maps. The following year another master took us for history and I gained 'O' level easily enough. Now, in the Sixth Form, I am still taking history. The master we have is a dilettante, newly down from university, but his knowledge is good and teaching skill immense. But I still shudder when I see Mr. Beaver striding down a corridor and feel pity for the second and third forms, ceaselessly drawing maps of battles and fearing cricket practice.

30. Describe a thunderstorm. **[30 min.]**

Plan.

1. Day—fine.
2. Beginning of the storm.
3. Thunder overhead.
4. Rain.
5. After the storm.

The day was very hot and overhead the mid afternoon sun bore down from a deep blue sky. Far away there were large, fleecy clouds spilling upwards perhaps five or six miles high and growing like some gigantic fungus.

Whisps of cloud drifted across the sun which took away the harshness so that the whole sky was bathed in yellow flowing light. The air, which had been crisp and dry turned slowly and imperceptibly sultry. It seemed as if one could gather it up in armfuls it was so moist and sticky. The slight breeze that had been blowing all day dropped and the leaves hung listless and still. The birds stopped singing and huddled in the trees and bushes waiting. At first the thunder was insignificant, no more than a rumbling in the distance, an occasional odd flash of lightning. The air was dead and static and it was harder to breathe.

The thunder once far away, was suddenly overhead, and blue light flashed across the sky. A dog whimpered and a crowd of swallows flew into the air, only to settle again on the telegraph wire. More lightening followed. Some flashed across the sky, other belts forked towards the ground, white blue, purple yellow streaks of energy. One must have struck a power cable for all the lights in the house went out. The thunder kept up an incessant rumble, punctuated by deafening rolls of noise.

When the rain came, it fell in large, elongated drops that bounced on the road. Soon puddles formed, then linked up with other puddles and the road outside was awash with a quarter of an inch of water, all within a space of fifteen minutes. The drains could not cope and the water piled up and spread from the roadway into the gardens. Flotsam from the gutters floated past.

The rain stopped as abruptly as it had started. The roads steamed and a breeze stirred the leaves of the trees. The air smelled and felt fresher. The sky was calm, washed clean by the rain.

31. Write an essay on an important scientific discovery.
[1 hour]

Plan.

1. Scotland in the sixteenth century.
2. Discovery of logarithms: present day view.
3. Introduce Napier. Background. Education.
4. Age in which he lived. Showed scientific interest in various fields.
5. Main work and earlier developments.
6. Napier's overall success.

Scotland enjoyed a brief Renaissance in the late fourteenth and early fifteenth centuries with the border poets, notably Dunbar. In the mid-sixteenth century her culture lapsed, and the country was once more a place for barbaric, clannish feuds. This obscurantism was to continue for most of the seventeenth century, and not until the eighteenth century were Scottish engineers to begin to make a name for themselves. Yet, in one of the most chaotic periods of Scottish history, the country was to produce a mathematician who ranks with Archimedes, Newton and Albert Einstein.

Speaking at the Tercentenary Celebrations of his birth, Lord Moulton said:

> 'No previous work had led up to it, nothing had foreshadowed it or heralded its arrival. It stands isolated, breaking in upon human thought abruptly, without borrowing from the work of other intellects or following known lines of mathematical thought'.

The man was John Napier of Merchiston and his discovery was the principle and compilation of the mathematical tables every schoolboy knows today as 'logs'.

From 1550 to 1617, Napier was the eighth Lord to occupy the family seat. His ancestors had been hereditary landowners in Dunbartonshire and Stirlingshire and had ably fulfilled their public service duties. Napiers had fallen in the battles of Sauchie-burn. Flodden and Pinkie; several members of the family had been Provosts of Edinburgh and Napier's father had been master of the mint to James VI. John Napier's early life was spent studying. In 1563 he entered St. Andrew's University where he studied philosophy but did not complete a degree. He then studied at the Sorbonne University in Paris and met many of the leading intellectuals of his age. He returned to Scotland, but here he broke with family tradition. Instead of pursuing his career as a courtier, as many of his forbears had done, he devoted himself to study.

Violent religious controversy arose when the merits of Protestantism and Roman Catholicism, as the national religion for Scotland were discussed. Napier, a firm believer in Knox's doctrine, contributed a pamphlet to the arguments. He also busied himself with the invention of a chariot which could be wheeled rapidly about and which could carry cannon. Although it aroused interest it was never implemented. Again, Napier took part in the current enthusiasm for agriculture and experimented with fertilisers. Even water divining attracted him, and he was often seen at night, carrying a forked stick and accompanied by a black dog. Local people accused him of witchcraft, but fortunately the charges were not pressed, otherwise dog and genius could have ended their days on a bonfire.

It is not recorded how long he took to work out the logarithm tables. Even as a young man Napier probably knew of the difficulties encountered by mathematicians when they tried to multiply or divide large numbers. The Indians and Arabs had developed rudimentary tables, but these were difficult to manipulate. Sixteenth century astronomers had encountered great difficulties and were held up to some extent because of the laborious nature of the calculations. Napier highlighted this problem in his book, 'Mirifici Logarithorum Canonis Descritio' presented to an amazed intellectual world in 1614. He wrote:

> 'Seeing there is nothing (right well beloved students of mathematics) nor so troublesome to mathematical practice, than that doth molest and hinder calculations than the multiplications, divisions, square and cubical extractions of great numbers, which besides the tedious expense of time are for the most part subject to many slipping errors . . . . I found at length some excellent rules'.

These 'excellent brief rules' ran to thirty seven pages of description and ninety pages of tables. These Napier had compiled and tested over a lifetime. The basic idea of logarithms is said to have been glimpsed by Archimedes and Euclid. To Napier, however, falls the honour of implementing these ideas. For his achievement Napier became famous. His tables were labour saving, and, to the seventeenth century scientific revolution they were vital. Logarithms consolidated the work of past mathematicians and gave the machinery for calculating that Kepler, Galileo and Newton were to need.

32. Write a review of a book you enjoyed. [1 hour]

Plan.

1. Book and author.
2. Early experiences.
3. Difficulties—illness.
4. Everyday life—guerilla fighters.
5. Guerilla beliefs. Training.
6. Personal amusements.
7. Contacts with other commandos.
8. Capture and escape.
9. Submarine pick up.
10. Final reaction.

'The Jungle is Neutral' by F. Spencer Chapman tells how the author survived for three years, five months in the Malayan jungle. In 1941 Chapman was a specialist in jungle and guerrilla warfare. At that time Staff Officers had not realised the potential that such units would have against the Japanese. Only with the capture of the Malayan Peninsula a reality and with the fall of Singapore imminent was Chapman given the orders to organise resistance movements to the occupying Japanese.

In the chapter 'The Mad Fortnight' the author describes how he and a few companions, constantly in peril from superior numbers with better equipment, ambushed Japanese convoys and trains. He soon realised, however, that these small scale attacks were of little value and that at best they would only achieve marginal results. The best plan was to link up with Chinese guerrilla forces and try to organise effective resistance groups which could take part in co-ordinated attacks. Finally Chapman hoped to be able to leave Malaya with local knowledge and go to Ceylon where he could retrain other groups and lead them back with proper equipment.

A good plan if it could be put into practice, Chapman had to survive in the jungle until it could be realised. These years were to be a time of endless worries, doubts, hopes and disappointments. Tropical fever and malaria were constant threats. These illnesses he accepted with a certain stoicism. Of one serious illness he writes:

> 'We reached John's house and I collapsed with high fever and pneumonia, then was visited with an attack of dysentery . . . luckily there were some sluphathiazole tablets in my medical set, and it was due to these that I did not die of pneumonia'.

On two occasions Chapman was wounded. The surgical equipment of his Chinese companions was so primitive that a half inch nut had to be extracted from his leg with a bamboo probe. All this

Chapman accepted.

Life in the jungle was lived in a state of bored nervousness. Chapman shared his guerrilla companions' fear of a surprise attack. With most of their equipment captured and with inadequate food supplies, life was dull and demoralising. Contact with other groups was made only under great difficulty and suspicion amongst the various groups was strong. Chapman was an outsider, part of a vanquished race, whose presence was accepted but not thought especially useful.

Chapman, a professional soldier and expert in his own field, found the guerrilla troops particularly inept at organising attacks, handling men, or planning ahead. Instead, they seemed to be more concerned with the education of their followers and the setting up of a government after the war. Camp life followed a monotonous routine and to prevent Chapman learning the language and so being able to understand everything that was said, he was given different teachers who spoke different dialects. To amuse himself Chapman would teach the guerrillas jungle warfare. In one camp he had to teach the men in the morning and then the officers in the afternoon so that the men did not know more than their equally ignorant officers. Occasionally concerts were held where communist party songs, local folk songs and Chapman's ability to yodel were called for..

In difficult circumstances Chapman undoubtedly survived through sheer will power and determination. Hunting took up a great deal of his time and he often made himself indispensible by killing fresh game. A specialist in jungle navigation, he used to purposely lose himself just to be able to find his way back to camp again. Despite these activities, bad health at times threatened to wear him down, as did the lack of news. Japanese papers were strongly propagandist and told of the Allies defeat everywhere. Finally the camps themselves were noisy, there appears to have been a constant racket going on all the time.

To his delight the Jungle Training School in Colombo sent a commando force. Chapman was heard of and met Davis and Broome, the former hard working, the latter lazy but very intelligent. Regrettably, however, their plan failed, for a rendezvous with a submarine was not achieved, and the information that they had collected could not be sent back to Head Quarters.

Chapman then set out to search for another white man in the jungle, Noone, and was captured by a Japanese patrol. He escaped by spectacularly racing down a river bed and through some rapids. A camp was then established with three Englishmen and a Chinese radio operator. After weeks of trial and error with first an improvised radio receiver and then a transmitter, a message was sent back to Ceylon, telling of the whereabouts of the various resistance groups. Great excitement was felt when Liberator bombers came over and parachuted supplies to the men below.

Arrangements were made to take Chapman out by submarine and great suspense builds up as one wonders, by this stage in the book, whether there will be another setback and failure. However, for once all went well with Chapman and he found himself back at his headquarters and promoted to Colonel. However, once he had had some time to recover, and had given his detailed information to his fellow officers he was parachuted into Malaya and was there when the war ended. He aided in the setting up of a new administration and would have had his group prepared, had the Japanese made any last stand.

Reading 'The Jungle is Neutral' one has the same admiration for the author as one has for T. E. Lawrence who wrote 'Seven Pillars of Wisdom' the great book of the First World War. Chapman is not so profound or introspective as his predecessor but nevertheless his narrative holds one in-suspense at times and in admiration all the time. One's final reaction is still—how did he do it?

33. 'The cinema is doomed because it cannot compete with television'. Comment. [1 hour]

Plan.

1. First effects of television.
2. Rebirth of the cinema.
3. Situation of television—easy incomes.
4. Television . . freedom for cinema.
5. Film develops new techniques.
6. Epic films.
7. New image of cinema.
8. Pilkington.
9. Conclusion.

When television appeared in the postwar years many people cheerfully acknowledged that the cinema was doomed and that it could not compete with the television screen. Television was new, its material original: while the cinemas were old, many of the buildings were draughty and the prices were high. Many of the traditional 'flea pit' cinemas did close. Questions in Parliament were asked and many people showed a concern fostered by hindsight.

What all the critics and most of the public did not realise was the power that the cinema was to gain in the years from 1955-1965. The cinema of the nineteen twenties and thirties rarely produced good films. Directors, actors and managers knew that the public wanted 'light entertainment' and 'escapist' films. People wanted to go to the cinema to live in a dream land for three hours, and perhaps to have a good weep over stories marked by their tedium of dialogue and their innocence of subject.

Technically, television production is much simpler than film making. Fewer people are involved, the equipment needed is easier to operate and the revenue from licences and advertising brings in a vast income. People must pay for licences, manufacturers cannot afford not to advertise, hence the money to finance television is quickly earned. A television producer does not have to worry greatly over his box office. People live in houses, television presides and people watch.

The film producers and directors of Europe, Britain and Hollywood were aware of this. However, they were aware also that they gained their freedom and could develop films of a higher level than 'Lassie Come Home'. The subsidised cinemas of the Iron Curtain Countries and experimental films from countries such as Sweden, France and Italy began to demonstrate new and startling techniques. 'Ashes and Diamonds', 'The Seventh Seal' and 'Umberto D' depended for their success on the large cinema screen and the dramatic suspense that a collective audience builds up.

Again film directors and producers knew that there would be no interruptions due to 'Mum' getting up to make tea when their films were showing. They knew also that television was hard work and would become even harder as time went on. In Britain, almost twenty hours of television has to be produced each day. By contrast, a big film company can spend millions of pounds and take two years to make a film. Television actors are seldom known by the public, the cast in a good film can gain international reputation overnight. With a keen sense of financial expertise and using men and women with talents and artistic vision, the cinema went to work to develop new and exciting techniques.

Whilst film executives happily sold old films, guaranteed to turn people ill with boredom, to the television companies, the film directors bought up the best talents that television was producing, besides discovering their own actors and actresses. The influence of the Iron Curtain, and Continental films was insufficient to swing the balance from television to cinema until Hollywood started to produce film epics such as 'The Robe', 'The Ten Commandments' and 'The Bible' sequences.

The wave of experimentation with new films and new themes, for suitable adult audiences led to many failures. However, once the successes were winnowed from the failures the cinema was in a formidable position. New screens, exciting new subjects and a keen knowledge that failure would cost millions led the cinema industry onwards. People became aware in Britain that the cinema was going through a revival when 'Bridge on the River Kwai' and the 'hard' Northern films 'Saturday Night and Sunday Morning', 'Look Back in Anger', 'A Kind of Loving' and 'A Taste of Honey' appeared.

It was at about the same time that the television industry was languishing under the criticisms made by the Pilkington Commission's enquiry. To say the least, the comments were not favourable. Also, many people, once the novelty wore off television, were turning back to the cinema. Once in the cinemas, modernised and with new and larger screens, people knew that a seventeen, twenty one, or even twenty five inch screen could not compete with the cinemas' efforts. Also live theatres were closing. By widening the facilities available at cinemas, for example opening bars, going to the cinema became an occasion and some theatre-goers switched their habits.

For the cinema to extricate itself from the bad and incompetent habits it had fallen into in the nineteen thirties, and to eliminate television as a rival was a difficult task. Old ideas had to go. Once the cinema industry achieved this it has become unsurpassed. "West Side Story', 'Zulu', 'Tom Jones,' 'Lawrence of Arabia' and 'Arabesque' attests to this.

34. Write an essay about an inventor whom you would like to have known. [1½ hours]

Plan.

1. Modesty of James Watt.
2. Childhood.
3. Did not have to go to work in childhood.
4. Death of his father.
5. London.
6. Instrument maker.
7. First interest in steam engine.
8. Surveyor.
9. Early association with Matthew Boulton.
10. Death of wife. Built first engine.
11. First engine installed.
12. Remarriage. Years of success.
13. Comments on his work from a Victorian.
14. Comments on his failure to build a locomotive.
15. An old man.

Watt's own words, 'I have no great experience and am not enterprising, seldom choosing to attempt things that are great or new' speak for the modesty of the man who built the first true steam engine. James Watt, born into a skilled artisan's home in 1736, was to give the emerging industrial revolution its power to build metal presses, to drive textile mills and to drain the deeper pits. True, the more famous Stephenson team built the first locomotive, but Watt mastered the perplexing problem of harnessing steam to drive pistons.

Watt's life was not easy. He suffered from migraine and toothache to such an extent that as a child he would try to start conversations late at night so that he would not have to go to bed and suffer alone. Unlike most children he had a great deal to talk about for he had a flare for mathematics and enjoyed reading books about scientific phenomena and natural philosophy. The young James was both intelligent and creative. One recorded instant of this occurred when he was staying with his aunt. The lady became very irritated after the child had held a spoon over the spout of a steaming kettle and had carefully observed its movements due to the pressure of the steam.

For an age when there was no state education Watt was fortunate in that he did not work until he was eighteen. Instead, he helped his father and was allowed to pursue his own interests. So, in his most formative years he had the basic grounding for a technologist—that of empiricism. The years that were to follow were to test his early patience and interests to the utmost.

His relatively sheltered life came to an abrupt end. Severe financial losses in his father's business meant that James and his elder brother had to earn their own livings. His brother went to sea and was drowned; James went to Glasgow and tried to enter the restrictive trade of the scientific instrument makers. No one would give him an apprenticeship at a reasonable cost and he was forced to work for a man who undertook to instruct him for twenty guineas a year. He worked twelve hours a day, but so eager and impecunious was Watt that he worked extra overtime hours for a pittance. Within a few months he could make his living as a journeyman. Like many young men before him he trekked to London to seek fortune and success.

Shortly after his arrival in London he heard of the death of his beloved mother. Combined with his migraine, toothache, and the long hours of work, Watt nearly suffered a nervous breakdown. He returned to Scotland and hoped to set up his own shop in Glasgow. Local hostility and monopolistic practices stopped this. In his unending stream of ill luck there was one chance given him.

He was appointed as official instrument maker to Glasgow University. Although he made little money from this he gained a reputation as a talented young man. With the hard earned seventy pounds made over two years from the University he took on workmen and set out to break the 'closed shop' practices in Glasgow by producing articles of the same quality but far cheaper than had hitherto been offered. Shrewd sea captains soon purchased his nautical instruments and Watt had a living to hand. He also married a cousin capable of helping and soothing him in his difficulties when physical pain wore him down.

Perhaps someone else would have built the first steam engine, had not Watt been given a model of the atmospheric engine, built in 1709 by Newcomen. This engine was both wasteful and inefficient. It could only be used at pit heads where there was a plentiful supply of coal. Watt started work in 1761. In 1763 he built the first model of a modern steam engine from a syringe and pieces of scrap. He had the confidence to find a loan of one thousand pounds to build full scale model engines but he was dogged with failure , for the science of metallurgy in Scotland was insufficiently developed to be able to produce accurate steam joints. Worry and strain led him to sell two thirds of the patent rights to a Doctor Roebuck so as to enable him meet his financial difficulties.

Driven to find extra money he took up road survey work. Succeeding at this he was called to London to sit on a parliamentary commission. While he found politicians 'muddle headed' he also found his way to the Soho iron works of Boulton which had recently been built in Birmingham. Although on his first visit to the iron works, Boulton was away, his deputy, Dr. Small, was impressed by the nervous young Scot.

In the following year, 1768, the two men, Boulton and Watt, whose combined names were to represent one of the largest engineering firms of the nineteenth century, met. Opposite in almost everything—Boulton was a clever business man and had married an heiress and lived, if not in the grand manner then in a manner far above Watt—they were immediately impressed by each other. Immediately workshops were set up to help Watt develop his engine but circumstances were once more against Watt. Dr. Roebuck refused to allow the engine, in which he had a two thirds share to be developed. Adamantly he refused Boulton's generous offers.

Quietly Watt went back to his survey work. One day, in 1773 he was summoned from his work, rushed home and found that his wife had died in childbirth. Bereaved, frustrated in his work, and with two young children to support Watt was intensely depressed. However, if there are turning points in life, one came now for Watt. Dr. Roebuck went bankrupt: amongst his assets were the rights for the steam engine—in the market was Matthew Boulton. The great team had started. 'Mad Iron' Wilkinson—the gentleman who designed an iron coffin for himself—could produce the valves that had bedevilled the earlier attempts. The first engine was built and the first orders came in, from the tin miners of Cornwall.

To aid Watt install the engine in Cornwall another young Scot, Murdoch, was engaged. He was a practical man in every sense. If the Cornish miners argued he could brawl with several of them, usually winning, and then could get on with the job before him, and command their respect. Other successes followed.

Watt remarried and lived on the outskirts of Birmingham. For ten years modifications were made on the steam engine. Also the time was found to build a copying machine, the forerunner of the typewriter, and also a new method of bleaching textiles was evolved.

Then, in 1781, came the development that was to mobilise the industrial world—a rotary engine which could turn machinery was developed. One enthusiast wrote:

> 'It can engrave a seal, and crush masses of obdurate metal before it; draw out, without breaking, a thread as fine as gossamer, and lift a ship of war like a bauble in the air. It can embroider muslin and forge anchors, cut steel into ribbons and impel loaded vessels against the fury of the winds and waves . . . . It would be difficult to estimate the value of the benefits which these inventions have conferred . . . They have increased in-

definitely the masses of human comforts and enjoyments and rendered cheap and accessible, all over the world, the materials of wealth and prosperity'.

Purple in style, the contemporary commentator's words were true. The technological developments which have carried the world to where it is today—for better or for worse—had begun.

In the success story of his later years several further points arise. The great but modest inventor did not build a locomotive—also the patent rights checked others from trying until 1800 and by then the Napoleonic Wars left little available cash for 'hare brained' inventions.

Whatever Watt did for the world he appears at all times a humane and patient man. He never forgot from whence he had come, a humble Scottish background. Consequently, he left large sums of money to help those from similar circumstances. Finally, as he had suffered in his early life he was to suffer once more. Only one of his sons survived him: his great friend and supporter Boulton died to leave Watt a lonely old man. Watt never sought fame and endured great pain in his life: a part of his achievement was to overcome this and a part to develop something new. For these reasons he would have been an intriguing person to know.

35. Is space research and travel a waste of time and money, or will it one day be of value to mankind? [1 hour]

Plan.

1. Popular image of space travel.
2. Skills needed.
3. Details about space engineering.
4. Research.
5. By-products.
6. Other urgent priorities.
7. Assessment.

For years, the image of space travel was one of unparalleled journeys, the exploration of new planets and of battles with green eyed monsters. After the early successful manned flights by Russian and American cosmonauts, a blasé and flippant attitude towards landing on the moon developed. 1970 was given as the target date. This date was beaten by several months when the Americans first set foot on the moon at the beginning of 1969. In 1967 the world mourned the death of four cosmonauts, three suffocated and subsequently burned in an explosion at Cape Kennedy; the fourth, a Russian, was killed when his capsule's breaking and descent parachutes failed to open. With anything new there is bound to be risk and danger, but the untimely death of four brave men accentuates the magnitude and difficulties which will be encountered in exploring space.

Immense skill and effort are needed. Electronic control systems, meaningless to the layman, have to be packed into capsules not much larger than a small car. In these same capsules room has to be found for spacemen. To track the flight of space vehicles the Americans have had to build radio stations across the globe.

Behind a space flight lies much work and effort. New metals and fuels have had to be developed. Casing fabrics have to stand up to the heating effects caused by friction as space capsules enter the earth's atmosphere travelling at twenty thousand miles an hour. Volatile but controlled fuels have to be used to lift a giant rocket from its launching pad and to boost its speed to eleven miles a second so that it can leave the earth's atmosphere. On the ground massive fortifications have to be built to launch a rocket. The blast pad for a large rocket needs the same amount of concrete and steel needed to build eighty miles of motorway.

In the universities of the world, and in some of the giant industrial corporations, teams of highly trained mathematicians, physicists, engineers, chemists and biologists are seeking answers to the problems raised by space travel. A conservative estimate would indicate that four million people are directly engaged in building rockets. Also there are millions of men ancillary to the major projects. However, numbers become meaningless, especially when one is told that the space research cost x billion dollars or y billion roubles in any given year. What cannot be computed is the amount of resources that a nation is using up, in the form of raw materials, industrial plant and skilled manpower. Behind the propaganda lies harsh economic facts, often these are ignored because the world's giants, the U.S.S.R. and the U.S.A., are ideologically committed to the space race. Prestige is at stake. Also there is a certain military strategic advantage to be had in possessing the most sophisticated rockets. The present day rockets were developed from the German ones of World War II. One has to be sceptical as to whether America and Russia are dedicated to science or vanity, or driven on by fear.

Only a rabid anti-American or anti-Soviet would say that no good would come from the research that is being put into space travel. Countless new processes and endless data have been discovered in the last ten years. In a few years time products could appear on the market which have been evolved from the discoveries of the information gleaned in seeking answers to the problem of space travel. Already a pyrex dish is on the market. It has been developed from heat resistant materials used in space research vehicles and can be taken from the refrigerator to hot cooking stove. It is unkind, but relevant to quote an American sceptic, who commented that it was the most expensive dish ever designed.

Against the background of scientific and technocratic expertise, supported by a largely blasé public, momentarily subdued, other world problems tend to be eclipsed. Several years ago the 'Observer' showed a cartoon which emphasised one of the morals of space travel. Over the heads of two starving human beings in Asia or Africa flew a space capsule. Beneath the line drawing the words 'They fly faster than food' appeared. An American would justly point out that since 1945 a thousand pounds for every man, woman and child has been given in the form of foreign aid to underdeveloped countries. However, there remains much more work in this world, on this planet, still to be done. At home America is faced with serious problems which could benefit from financial help and technical expertise. Similarly, Russia has immense social problems centred around the still relatively low standard of living many of her people endure.

Perhaps it is judicious to end with the words of Isaac Newton, when he reviewed the popular attitude towards his own achievements. He said, 'I know not what the world may think of my labours'.

36. A famous explorer. **[1 hour]**

Plan.

1. Early life of Magellan.
2. Courtier's life.
3. Keen interest in navigation due to work of Prince Henry.
4. Magellan volunteers to join an expedition.
5. Hazards of seamanship and navigation.
6. Successes in India. Fame in Portugal.
7. Return to the East Indies. Public disgrace because of bribery accusation.
8. Secret plans to sail for Spain as Columbus before him had done.
9. Voyage receives backing: starts out. Rebellion in South America.
10. Ships find a way through the Straits of Magellan. Pacific crossing.
11. Death in the Phillippines.

If Magellan had not come from one of the wealthier and noble families of Portugal he would have eked out a nondescript life in the mountains. He never saw the ocean till he was a teenager. Instead as a child he hunted, rode and tracked through the mountains of Northern Portugal. As a child he showed the fearlessness, tenacity, independence and stubbornness that was to stand him in good stead later when he had to sail a small and leaking vessel from the Iberian Peninsula, round the tip of South America and into the Phillippines.

Since he was of noble birth, Magellan eventually received a courtier's education. In 1443, aged thirteen, he set out for the court of Queen Eleanora. Immediately he found the life—cosmopolitan, urbane and splendid—exciting. In Lisbon the Parochialism of the mountains was far away and all around him was the current infectious enthusiasm for exploration.

Prince Henry the Navigator's charter of the West African court bequeathed a strong sense of seamanship and exploration to the Portuguese. Training schools existed to equip and instruct officers and men for the voyages of discovery. In 1487 Bartholomew Diaz had rounded the Cape of Good Hope, while Columbus, flying Spanish colours, had discovered America. While a courtier, aged 18, the exciting news reached Magellan that Vasco de Gama had discovered India.

Untrained in the lore of the sea, and well established at court, Magellan answered de Gama's appeal, in 1504, for sailors to equip a further expedition to India. Life expectancy was slight, five out of six sailors died of disease or drowning. To make things even more harsh, Magellan enrolled at the Belem Naval school, on the Tagus, as an ordinary seaman.

Magellan was aware of the difficulties he would have to face. He left his estates to his sister Teresa, should he die, and sailed with the fleet in March 1505. Seamanship, despite training, was poor. One captain had to hold up a bunch of garlic when he wanted his helmsman to turn to port, and a bunch of onions for starboard, because he found his nautical commands were incomprehensible. In the first few weeks one ship was lost. The tedium of the long journey was broken by several skirmishes, the combined force of sailors and troops fought with the Moors for fortresses on the African coast. Some ships were left to patrol African waters, whilst the rest sailed on, eventually reaching India in 1606.

The relations with the Indian Princes were good, but the Arab traders, who had previously enjoyed a monopoly, bitterly resented the Portuguese. In March, 1506, barely two months after his arrival, Magellan and his compatriots found themselves with fifteen ships, having to engage a fleet of more than two hundred. The Portuguese, with superior fire power won. Encouraged by success the squadron sailed on across the Indian ocean to reach the coveted spice islands of Indonesia. The wily ruler resented the intruders and when a coup was attempted Magellan distinguished himself in the fighting. He returned to Portugal, after having travelled half way round the world, to find himself lionised and honoured.

In 1513 he was back once more in the Malacca Straits. However, his second trip was to be the turning point in his career. Rivalries and jealousies ran strong in the Portuguese court and Magellan was accused of profiteering. He returned once more to Portugal to clear his name, only to find that the monarch publicly rebuffed him. Determined to prove himself and spite his country he resolved to offer his services to Spain in a projected attempt to find a route to the Far East around the Americas.

For two years he studied in secret. He took a young and temperamental astronomer, Faleiro, into his trust, and between them they planned the voyage. Once his plans were made Magellan clandestinely travelled to Seville. Aged thirty seven, unknown and dishonoured by his own country, the explorer sought help. Luckily he met Diego Barbosa, a fellow ex-patriate, and through him gained an audience with Charles V. The Spanish monarch agreed to sponsor his voyage and placed five worn out vessels at his command.

The epic voyage began in 1519. In March of 1520 he contacted the natives of the Argentine, whom he named Patagonians because they resembled bears. He had to quell an insurrection by four of his captains, in the pay of the Portuguese court. Magellan was ruthless. One man he had flayed to death, another was stabbed, while the remaining two were driven into the interior to take their chance amongst the Patagonians, who had eventually proved hostile.

The Straits of Magellan, separating Tierra del Fuego from the South American mainland, were navigated more by good luck than good management. Two ships were driven into them in a storm. Magellan later followed. One of his captains, having lost faith in the expedition, turned back for Spain. On 28th November, 1520, Magellan and three ships entered the Pacific Ocean, the first recorded Europeans to do so. Ahead lay three months and twenty days sailing. Fresh food supplies were low and what remained was rotten, for as a diarist records 'the biscuit we were eating was nothing but dust and worms . . . the water we were obliged to drink was equally putrid and offensive. We were even so far reduced to eat pieces of leather with which the main yard was covered'. Scurvy broke out and many men suffered torments from broken gums and itching skin. At last the small flotilla reached the Phillippines.

Here, for the leader, one of the greatest voyages in history was to end. The King claimed certain dues and Magellan refused. Threatened with violence, the native King appeared pacified, but he then put an army of 1,500 against Magellan and his tired crew. In the battle Magellan was killed. However, he had reached the Phillippines sailing round Africa a few years before, he had now reached the same islands by sailing round South America. To him falls the honour of being the first man to sail round the world. For another fifty years no one sought to emulate his achievement.

37. Describe the uniform or clothing worn and the equipment used by one of the following—a hockey goal keeper, a nurse, a mountaineer, a wicket keeper. [30 min.]

Plan.

1. Introduction—How his dress is like that of other cricketers.
2. Description of his task, therefore need for padding.
3. Protection for hands.
4. Protection for legs.

A wicket keeper is dressed in the usual white flannels, shirt and jersey that all members of a cricket team wear. Also he wears a peaked cap, in the colours of his team. On his feet are cricketing boots, normally made of white leather.

His job is not an enviable one. He has to stand or squat behind the stumps and stop any balls that the batsman misses. If he fails, the batsman may snatch valuable runs. Also he must be ready to take catches that the batsman might inadvertently give. Finally, he must catch the balls thrown in by the fielders so as to be able to knock the bails off the wicket before a running batsman regains the crease. Naturally, with so much contact with fast moving, hard leather or cork cricket balls he must be well padded to save himself from injuries or bruises. Therefore unlike the rest of the fielding side at cricket, he must wear gloves and leg pads.

The gloves are strongly reinforced. They have a heavy gauntlet which extends above the wrist and up about five inches of the fore-arm. The back of the gloves are strengthened with pieces of cane, sewn in beneath the surface. These canes deflect the worst blows from a ball rising over the stumps at perhaps forty or fifty miles an hour. The fingers of the gloves are also strengthened with rubber and leather padding. Similarly, the thumb, which can easily be dis-jointed, has to be well protected. Only the palms of the gloves are soft and supple, for the wicket keeper's job is to catch swiftly flying balls.

The legs are shielded by heavy pads which come within a few inches of the groin. These protective pads have horizontal, corru-gated ribs, above and below the knee. At the knee itself the ribs extend horizontally around the knee cap. The pads are made out of white canvas. Cane or plastic is used for the ribs. Straps hold the pads in place. On a normal pad there are three straps, one at the ankle bone, one below the knee and one above the knee. Equipped like this, the wicketkeeper is ready to take the field.

38. 'Some see the motor car as a miraculous invention: others see it as man's greatest misfortune yet'. Discuss. [1 hour]

Plan.

1. Human interest in travel.
2. Freedom of movement.
3. Motor industry — jobs.
4. Shipbuilding.
5. Leisure activities.
6. Boost to construction industries.
7. Lethal weapon.
8. Legislation to control the use of cars.
9. Adaptability.

Many classic English novels, such as 'Humphrey Clinker', 'Redgauntlet', 'Nicholas Nickleby' and 'North and South' describe the remoter parts of the British Isles with the enthusiasm usually reserved for books of genuine exploration in the Amazon rainforest or the jungles of Borneo. Few writers employ this technique today. Up until 1850, many people lived in total ignorance of their own country. Railways first helped break down the parochial nature of English life. However, the motor car has proved the greatest means of travel yet for the individual. Writers seldom mention local detail because they are aware that their readers are likely to be familiar with the British Isles. In some books, such as 'I like it here' by Kingsley Amis a good knowledge of the Continent is also presupposed. Every year more motorists venture further afield, both in Britain and on the Continent.

Freedom of movement is a great benefit to all who can enjoy it. Sundays become interesting, once people can get away from their own homes. Because car owners are able to travel a number of miles to work each day, they can choose where they want to live and bring up their families. Similarly, women are free to escape from their homes for an evening or an afternoon to visit friends and attend social functions. Even teenagers, living in country areas, need cars to go to dances in neighbouring villages and towns.

Within fifty years motor manufacture has made itself one of the leading home and export industries. Factories at Luton, Dagenham, Oxford, Liverpool and Edinburgh employ thousands of engineers and semi-skilled workers. Whole towns depend for their livelihood on motor cars. Wages are high because productivity is high. Besides several hundred thousand workers directly employed in the motor industry, there is an army of ancillary workers. Practically every village has its own garage and service station. Many men, with a mixture of entrepreneurial skill and luck have carved out prosperous businesses for themselves.

The car's fuel consumption has aided ship building, in that tankers in ever increasing numbers and size, are called for to bring crude oil from the Middle East to Britain. Again, large numbers of men are employed in the refining and distribution of petrol and oil.

Because of the motor car, several leisure time activities have rapidly become popular. Motor racing and rally driving attract large numbers of spectators and participants. Caravanning and camping are made readily available if one has a car and is able to transport equipment easily. Coastal resorts again benefit from the influx of drivers and their families.

A boost to industry is given by the motor car. Construction firms are pressed more and more to expand their activities to build newer and bigger roads. Here the misfortunes that the car causes are first seen. Tens of thousands pass their driving test each year and add to the road congestion. Compton Mackenzie once humourously suggested that a newspaper headline of the future might tell of people starving to death in traffic jams. Although this is unlikely, one is aware of the problem he is highlighting. In many towns now traffic density exceeds one hundred cars a minute. Space for roads and car parks has to be found. Many city authorities are unable to keep abreast of the increased flow of traffic and many man hours and tempers are lost in traffic blocks. Large public expenditure, some of it paid for by the motorist, is involved in the construction of new roads. Some would argue that the engineering skill could be put to a more socially beneficial use by tackling the growing housing shortage, on the grounds that people can do without cars but they must have houses. Again, dual carriage ways, linking cities have to be built and often valuable farm land is commandeered for this purpose. This is inevitable, and will continue, if traffic increases. Many of the two lane motor roads of today may, in twenty or thirty years time, have to be rebuilt with three lanes.

A starker problem is presented by the road accident figures. Since the motor car was introduced into Britain, approximately a quarter of a million people have been killed. Currently, the present figure is seven thousand a year and many more are seriously injured. The personal grief caused by this loss is immense. However, there is a vast medical bill also in treating the injured. Hospital beds are occupied by the casualties, while some chronically sick people have to wait for treatment. Loss of wages leads to increased social service benefits for the taxpayer. Firms lose valuable and skilled operatives. Propaganda to reduce road accidents seems, as yet, to have had little effect. What many motorists do not realise is that while the car has given them freedom it has also presented them with a lethal weapon. Regrettably, reason is often lost by the normally calm individual when he finds himself behind the wheel of a vehicle. The car represents power and possession, and many motorists feel that they are able to behave as they please. Again, the car increases an individual's self importance and he becomes preoccupied by 'saving time'. Not surprisingly, the majority of accidents occur when overtaking.

In view of this one has to balance the personal and economic benefits brought by the car against the social distress and financial losses the car incurs on its owners and others. The car is not yet a disaster, but unless it is controlled it could become one. Safety standards in cars are still regrettably low. There is no effort at enforcing lane discipline as there is in America. Driving tests are often ludicrously simple. An aptitude test should be given to every potential motorist to see whether reactions and temperament are adequate to drive a vehicle. Perhaps comprehensive insurance cover should be abandoned, in as much as it relates to damage caused to a motorist's own vehicle. Drivers, aware that they might have to pay a bill for repairs running into hundreds of pounds if they were proved by a law court to have been at fault might be more cautious.

On the credit side for the motor car is its adaptability. There is great potential inherent within car ownership in that people can explore their world for themselves. Few would want to go back to the days of visiting by pony and trap. However, one does not want to live either in a world congested with traffic and polluted by exhaust gases. Perhaps it is too early to tell whether or not the car will be a bringer of universal misfortune.

39. Give an account of a great engineering feat that you have seen or read about. [1 hour]

Plan.

1. Proposal to build Trans-Siberian railway.
2. Factors contributing to construction.
3. Engineers.
4. Problems.
5. Lake Baikal — ferries.
6. Winter line across ice.
7. Labour force.
8. Work conditions.
9. Assessment.

In the 1880's a Mr. Dall proposed that a railed way should be built across Russia and that horses should pull the cars. He feared that a locomotive might set the timber alongside the line alight. His proposal was not seriously considered in the 1880's yet by 1904 the Trans-Siberian railway had been built crossing 4,600 miles of European and Asiatic Russia.

Numerous factors contributed to this achievement. Tsars, in the middle years of the nineteenth century, had opposed the building of railroads for they felt that better communications might lead to revolution. Nevertheless, some progress had been made in Eastern Russia. By 1890, however, the situation had changed for the then Tsar had designs in the Far East and saw Japan as a potential enemy. A line, for military and strategic, as well as economic reasons was needed. Western capitalists and investors were keen to help also. The great Canadian and American lines had shown their value by opening up the agricultural and mineral wealth of the continent, a similar result from the Russian venture was predicted.

Having ceremonially turned the first sod over, the Tsar and his ministers left the engineers and workers to carry on with the mammoth task. In European Russia it was not too difficult to raise a labour force. Manufactured equipment—rails, sleepers, and rolling stock—were available. The problems came when the engineers had to cross the Ural Mountains—soaring peaks with streams rushing through gorges. All observers admired the skill and ingenuity which went into the building of the bridges and permanent way, which crossed chasms and hugged the sheer sides of the gorges.

The real problem arose when the middle and far eastern sections had to be built. Local inhabitants were largely illiterate and often hostile. The labour force was unskilled and progress was slow. Methods were primitive. Heavy ballast could only be blasted from rock faces with the relatively new invention dynamite; then, painfully, it had to be smashed by men with sledge hammers. Lighter ballast was obtained by digging and then wheel barrowing the material to the site where it was needed. Many of the workers had not seen a wheel barrow until the western engineers introduced them. To add to the difficulties, proper roads did not exist and these made the transportation of essential goods even more difficult. Work was often stopped for five months in the winter as the land froze solid and defied pick axes and shovels. Finally, locally recruited or coerced labourers usually deserted during hay and harvest time.

Immense difficulties were encountered when Lake Baikal was reached. The deepest fresh water lake in the world, and surrounded by precipitous cliffs, it appeared it would take years to hack a route around the lake. Messrs. Armstrong and Whitworth of Newcastle upon Tyne were approached and a steamer to serve as a ferry was commissioned. The ship was built in six months, dismantled, crated, and shipped to St. Petersburg. There it was ferried by rail and on waterways to within a thousand miles of its destination The parts were then loaded on to mule trains and sledges—sever thousand pieces in all— and carted to the lake. Numerous items were lost in transit and there was no proper shipyard in which to assemble the steamer. Yet the engineers, Russian and others, succeeded, and the ship was successfully launched. A second ship, the 'Angora', was commissioned—it is still in service today, although White Guards sank the first ship during the Civil War following the Russian Revolution.

In summer these ships carried trains and their passengers across seventy miles of lake. In winter a railroad was hastily laid across the ice, and independent witnesses recorded that stations and signals were established. The dismemberment of this track was always left until the last possible moment, and one observer reports crossing the lake and noting a twenty kilometre split in the ice surface, parallel to the track. The ferry route was finally abandoned in 1904 when the Russian-Japanese war forced the military and strategic planners to build an alternative route because the ferries were not adequate for rapid troop movements.

Although the labour force was often poor and the conditions of work were extreme, the overall progress was impressive. However direct comparisons are misleading, for they cannot take into account all the considerations and factors which arose, the Trans-Siberian railway crept across the continent of Asia faster than the American and Canadian railroads did to make up 'Uncle Sam's Waistband'. The Americans took seven years to build 1,800 miles of railroad whereas the Russian and foreign engineers built almost three thousand miles of track in less than eight years. All over

Europe great interest was taken in the project and many considered it to be the eighth wonder of the world. Comments were made on the luxurious services available—Russian trains incorporated mobile churches, pullman saloons, gymnasia, travelling libraries, music rooms and ordinary carriages.

What many people did not know of were the conditions under which the men building the railroad lived and worked. Illiterate workers were recruited with the promise of high wages. They were badly fed and inadequately housed. A forced labour system, whereby a worker had to complete a certain amount of work in a set time or else forfeit his wages was introduced. Few worked for more than nominal wages, especially on the far eastern section of the railway. Camp followers—hard liquor sellers and gambling saloon proprietors—were protected by the authorities and took most of the money from the workers. Sundays saw a great number of men injured in brawls and falls. Thousands died because there were no proper medical facilities to check cholera, typhus and influenza outbreaks. Work conditions were so ill organised that men—whether illiterate labourers driven by famine or the lure of high wages, or convicts seeking one third remission of sentences—were injured at the rate of 368 per 'verst' of line constructed. As one Russian poet wrote later,

'Straight is the road, the cutting narrow,
Along the mileposts, the rails and the bridges,
How many Russian bones are buried . . . ?'

The answer would be that the total will never be known.

In considering the scope of the scheme the suffering undergone must be balanced against it. Some even doubted if the railroad fulfilled all its promises of financial gain. Critics said it was built for prestige and military reasons rather than for economic reasons. Despite these reservations, the railroad remains today, the biggest single feat of engineering in the nineteenth century. Perhaps it also represents what was best and worst in nineteenth century industrial civilisation, a vision which incorporated thinking on a scale approaching grandeur but which, at the same time, discounted human suffering.

40. Describe a small town or village which has interested you. [45 min.]

Plan.

1. Introduce and name town. Emphasise the contrasts.
2. Market place and castle.
3. New parts of the town.
4. People.
5. History.

No railway station poster or travel agents brochure will ever evoke the attractions of Richmond. Perched precariously on a steep, North Yorkshire hillside, overlooking the River Swale, Richmond is a town of contradictions. It has developed since the middle ages and ought to be a monstrosity of planning and mixed styles but there is a unity and dignity in the town rarely found elsewhere.

The market place has cobblestones, an ancient church, modern shop fronts and cars. In the background there is the castle, a gaunt, ruined Norman castle, designed as a fortress against marauding bands of Scots. Holiday makers scramble over it, and from its walls gaze down at the river two hundred feet below. Straggling down the hillside are cottages, built in the eighteenth century. Red pan tiles, walls of local brown stone and winding alleys make a strange, but harmonious contrast with the castle itself. Leading off from the market place are sedate Georgian terraces. The houses, three and four storeys high, recall a leisurely past. One can almost hear the clatter of horses and carriages in these narrow streets. In Richmond the old and new can exist, side by side. There is no clash, no disunity.

Above the old part of the town are the new housing estates reaching up the hillside. Sadly uniform, the modern houses give way to fern, heather and stone walls. Anywhere else they would be an eyesore. In Richmond, fortunately, they are dwarfed by the massive expanse of the Pennines, stretching endlessly away up the Swale valley.

Without people, no town would be interesting. In Richmond, people, like buildings, make a strange contrast. On market day droll shepherds, shrewd farmers, tradesmen and hawkers, clerical and manual workers, retired colonels and delicate old ladies mingle unobstrusively. A strange dash of glamour is added as troops from nearby Catterick Garrison walk about in their various uniforms, green caps for the infantry, black for the armoured corps, red for the cavalry. Occasionally, a convoy of military trucks or armoured cars passes through the town, heading for the large moorland training areas. The townspeople observe all this with a mild, but unexcited interest.

The town has had a varied history. Since Norman times it has suffered invasion, religious persecution, rebellion, a thriving lead mining industry, industrial depression and finally, the twentieth century. People in Richmond are accustomed to change and diversity. Life is accepted and lived in a quiet, purposeful fashion.

41. Tell a story, showing how you had an accident because you failed to take care. **[1 hour]**

Plan.

1. Mr. Amble. Knowledge of the safety precautions to be taken.
2. Knowledge of rock climbing.
3. Setting out alone.
4. Freedom.
5. Mist.
6. Falling.
7. Injured.
8. Delirium - unconsciousness.

Mr. Amble taught me all I knew about rock climbing and hill walking. He was very fat and weighed over eighteen stone and wore gold rimmed spectacles. At school he taught Latin and was nicknamed Crassus. He seemed a funny sort of person to have as a mountaineering coach but as a young man, in some remote era, he had been one of the world's most renowned Alpinists.

His lectures on climbing, illustrated with slides taken with a plate camera always ended with the words, 'Remember, boys, remember to take precautions. Accidents happen because people don't. Always take extra clothing in your pack, and don't forget your food and matches and never go out without a map and compass. Never climb on your own, because, boys, if you do, you'll have the mountain rescue teams looking for you and they might not be soon enough'. There then followed a tale, marked by its graphic details, of some party which had met an untimely death because they had not taken precautions. One party, climbing in the Urals in 1907 had, according to Mr. Amble, been devoured by the last large pack of European wolves. Long after Mr. Amble had left we all remembered what he used to say, because common sense was the keynote of his talks.

Ian and I had arranged to go climbing in the last Easter holiday before we left school. He failed to meet me in Keswick, as we had arranged. I was vexed because the weather, for April, was ideal, a thaw three weeks ago had eradicated all the snow and there was no hint of rain. Alone, I could not go rock climbing but hill walking was still a possibility. I set out to hike to the next youth hostel, thirteen miles away. Uneasily I remembered that Ian had been bringing the compass. Still, I had plenty of maps and the weather was clear.

Outside Keswick I left the road and began walking steadily up the steep Lake District hillsides. Scornfully I gazed on the insect-like cars creeping along the roads below, the victims of every traffic jam and road diversion. I was free. At sixteen hundred feet whole ranges of hills were visible. I sat down to eat my sandwiches, gazing at Lake Ullswater far off in the distance. It was strange that there were so few climbers and walkers about. I had the whole of the country to myself, with no one at all to bother me.

In the twenty minutes that it took to eat my sandwiches a few wraiths of distant clouds had transformed themselves into a swirling, dismal mist. I turned back, knowing that I was doing what Mr. Amble would have done. But, as I told myself, Mr. Amble would have never set off without a compass. I knew where I was from my maps. Unfortunately, in the mist I could not see where I was going.

It must have been about four in the afternoon when I slipped. the grass was damp and I was tired. I found myself sliding and slithering down a scree slope. Small stones rattled all around me but a large piece of rock broke my fall. When I tried to ease myself up I found it had broken my arm as well. The two extra sweaters in my rucksack were useless now because I could not put them on. Every time I tried, pain jumped from my left wrist, up my arm, into my shoulder and down through my ribs. I wriggled into as comfortable a position as I could find. I blew a whistle, part of Mr. Amble's 'essential equipment' until its sound and echo irritated me. I wondered which mountain rescue team would find me first. I was frightened, because I had seen no one and had told nobody where I had intended going.

I became very angry with Ian. If he had arrived then this would not have happened. It was his fault entirely, but it was I who lay injured in a remote rock gully somewhere between Keswick and Penrith. When I slipped I had known for an hour and a half that I was utterly lost, and, like a fool, had wandered and blundered about, hoping to get down safely. As abruptly as the mist had fallen it cleared again.

The stars sparkled icily down and a quarter moon shone palely. There was nothing to be seen, nothing to be heard. My arm, which had stopped hurting so much about half an hour after I fell started again. It was as if someone was picking small pieces of bone out with a pair of tweezers after heating them with a blowlamp. Then there were people all around me, shouting at me, telling me what a fool I had been, and with them there was Mr. Amble, reading his lecture sheet to us all. Then they all ran away. I had read of the symptoms. I was becoming delirious and would soon be unconscious. I made one last effort, blowing on the whistle as hard as I could. I waited for the echo, but heard, instead, a well modulated voice shouting back at me, 'Boys, never forget your map and compass and never go alone. If you do, the mountain rescue teams will be after you and they might not be soon enough'.

42. Write a story entitled 'My First Car'. [45 min.]

Plan.

1. Eccentricities of 'Ophelia'.
2. Attitude of police.
3. Other motorists.
4. Mutiny.
5. Deterioration.

I bought 'Ophelia' for ten pounds—in good running order I was told by the scrap iron dealer who sold her to me. Built in 1946, the car had everything that she should have had, including a ten year test certificate. Soon, she was the great interest and expense of my life. Learning to drive her was an endless tale of frustration and excitement. Seldom did the vehicle run for more than twenty minutes before it needed attention. Hill starts were the big problem as the car used to refuse to move and threatened to shake to bits. while Christopher, my instructor as well as school friend, screamed commands in my ear. Clouds of alarmingly black fumes poured from the exhaust in several places and often the car was filled with stinking smoke.

Police officers used to take a suspicious interest in the car and her occupants. We were rather noticeable, having painted the vehicle in lemon and purple. At first they did not believe what they saw, then they thought we were part of a touring circus; finally, they questioned us in detail about licences and insurances. Once they were certain that we were not breaking the law they were full of helpful advice as to the care of aged cars. Finally, they would roar off in their five thousand pound automobiles, leaving us to trundle along at a steady twenty-five miles per hour.

Other motorists were generally helpful. Even the occasional scornful jibe was often tempered by a nostalgic gleam as the driver remembered his first 'banger'. Lorry drivers were the most interested. They detected in us the signs of the underprivileged for our vehicle was in a worse condition than anything else on the road They would flash their lights, give us thumbs up signs, and, if stopped in traffic, yell friendly advice at us. One day a driver with a Glaswegian accent, stopped to help us and performed an apparent miracle with a piece of string and a nail.

Despite Ophelia's valiant service, however, I tried my test in a driving school vehicle. This must have insulted her for as soon as I had ripped off the 'L' plates she became unmanageable. She spluttered before starting and stopped half a mile down the road. Four mechanics diagnosed various remedies and some made ineffectual attempts to get her to go once more. All failed.

She stood, derelict and senile, for three months. A scrap merchant offered five pounds for her but for sentimental reasons I refused. Her coat gradually lost its glossy shine and became streaked and chipped. A back tyre collapsed. It was quite apparent that Ophelia was not going to survive the winter. Since her life with me had been precarious and eventful, I decided to give her a dramatic end. Christopher's birthday coincided with the anniversary of Guy Fawke's plot to destroy parliament. Ophelia was the principal foundation of the bonfire, with sticks and thorns, paper and refuse all around her. She burnt well and made a graceful skeleton. It seemed better that way than the indignity of the local junk yard.

43. Going to church. [1 hour]

Plan.

1. Attitudes to church going today.
2. Victorian attitudes.
3. Drama and ritual.
4. Dissatisfaction with newly acquired wealth.
5. Fear and ignorance.
6. Obligatory attendance.
7. Individual's decision.

To attend church regularly today is to invite criticism and ridicule; to many, church going has become synonymous with social climbing and snobbery. Some tediously complain that the senior churchmen ride in expensive cars and live in large houses. This, they argue, is remote from the Christian tenets of poverty and humility. Again, existentialists, Zen Buddhists, the flat earth society and other break away groups explain that the basis of Christianity is fallible, though when asked why this is so they are usually vague. Finally, one meets the science sixth former who goes into an erudite monologue about hydrogen, helium, nuclear fission, the atomic weight of iron, bodies exploding outwards, clouds of rock and dust and the growth of new planets saying therefore, 'Christianity is irrelevant'. Few critics have the high degree of intelligence, or the necessary knowledge to argue theological subtleties. Those who attend church today do so for simple, sincere reasons of their own. The church always was, and still is, a social meeting place. People go to revere a certain creed of values held by others.

In Victorian times the church was the foundation of family life, the bible the main reading material. It was usual to have a reserved family pew, husband and wife and their brood of children sat in the same places each week. Today, going to church still gives people a reason to wear their best clothes; the ladies their hats, the men their Sunday suits. The clergy in their dog collars, the buildings with their thick pillars, stone floors, poor central heating, hard wooden pews and rich stained glass windows are unchanged. And the twentieth century stays outside.

Worship is dramatised by its ritual. The building itself is designed to exalt the individual and take him outside himself. The various vestments worn by clergy and choir, the different altar cloths, the altar itself, and the music, all aid in dramatisation of belief. Reverence is induced through singing and prayers, while the sermon, delivered from the pulpit, will, from a good preacher expound in clear terms, those things that one has always vaguely known. Without drama and ritual, belief is more difficult to inculcate. The

Anglican and Roman Catholic Churches recognise this; hence religious worship is full of ceremony and tradition. The framework of the building adds to this tradition. Wars and those who died in them are remembered in sculpture. Commemorative plaques tell the life stories of people who worked for what they believed to be the common good. In the seventeenth and eighteenth centuries many people devoted their lives to helping the poor. In the nineteenth century it was fashionable for wealthy tradesmen to donate money to the church and be perpetuated by the laying of a stone. Indeed, many of these worthy citizens were buried within the church walls.

The nouveau riche of the twentieth century—those who have become very wealthy quickly in our slick society—are often dissatisfied with the materialism of the world today and have turned to religion. If they have found Christianity lacking they have built a faith around other gods or around ideas such as 'make peace not war' or 'make babies, not bombs'. There are others who still have nowhere to go in particular and take comfort from a free evening in a society that cares. Going to church provides an interval of escapism from the loneliness and everyday worries, a time in which they do not have to think. Again, people need to be told what to do. For many, the church offers an acceptable set of rules by which people can live. There is a desire in man to find a god, a superior being to worship. Superstition and fear have, in time, invested supernatural powers in the sun, moon, trees, rivers and man made idols. This kind of irrational feeling still leads some to church.

Fear and ignorance of life after death is a strong motive for church going especially among the aged who think their lives on earth are coming to an end. The condemned murderer in his cell seeks solace from the prison chaplain before execution. Life is sweet and the thought of everlasting life is sweeter.

Society sometimes makes attendance at church obligatory. For some it means a free meal and a bed for the night. Nurses, scouts and military personnel have church parades, judges pray for guidance before the start of a session and civic dignitaries attend before taking public office. At nine a.m., Christian children in schools try to concentrate on their prayers and hymn books. There are festivals and occasions in the year when people feel obliged to go to church such as Christmas Day, New Year's Eve, Ash Wednesday and Good Friday. Good Christians are expected to take communion and say confession. People find some comfort in burying their loved ones in consecrated soil with a minister of the church officiating and couples like the church to bless their union and christen their children.

The individual must make up his own mind about what he believes. It may be that religion fulfills the need to teach him that there is something beyond himself. Church attendance figures are not an entirely accurate guide to the extent of Christian feeling in the world. Some find the service out of touch with today's language and certain pronouncements on, for example, birth control and divorce unacceptable in their personal lives. Thus, many who would like to go to church do not. They find something lacking in the administration not the religion, the singer not the song. Finally, one goes to church because one enjoys it and feels that one has missed something in life by failing to go. Western civilisation has grown up around a series of Christian beliefs and these still seem valid to many in the world of today.

44. What are the threats to the future of wild life? How can these threats be avoided? [1 hour]

Plan.

1. Animals already extinct.
2. Hunters—sportsmen.
3. Hunters—commercial.
4. Population expansion and reduction of land available for animals.
5. Science and progress—side effects.
6. Chemicals and insecticides.
7. Need to realise the danger to wildlife.

The dodo, the American passenger pigeon and the blue antelope are now extinct. Sperm and blue whales, the European wolf, birds of paradise and rhinoceroses are likely to disappear in the next forty years. In England the pine marten, wild cat, polecat, otter and sparrow hawk are rarely found. In all cases man is responsible, directly or indirectly, for the disappearance of these and other animals.

Hunting threatens the survival of wildlife. Many men, women and children thoughtlessly kill and maim animals for pleasure. Some sportsmen specialise in collecting the heads and hides of already rare species. In this way the danger of extinction of these animals is increased. It is easy to suggest that a series of proscriptive laws be set up to protect these animals. But, without the co-operation of the public they would be unlikely to work. Instead, it is perhaps a better idea to stress to people the idea that animals have a right to live. Animals can be 'shot' with a camera as well as with a gun. A photographic record of a graceful bird or a rare animal is surely worth more than a glass case in the front hall.

Commercial hunting represents a further threat to wildlife and its existence. Many nations have vast whaling and trawling fleets. Inevitably, both whales and sea fish are threatened. Man scours the sea, killing most of what he takes out. As yet, few efforts have been made to farm the sea in the way that men farm the land. Year after year the whaling fleets break the quotas set up by an international board of control. While man needs the products of whales and fish, his policy, which could be described as one of systematic extermination, is short sighted. If the whale is to be harpooned into history no one will gain. For sea fish the prospect is less bleak. Under the influence of Cousteau's work, some nations are experimenting with 'fish farms'. Also, the extension of territorial waters may give some protection against over fishing. Man has the answer within his grasp—regulated controls—it is up to men and nations to make these controls work.

On land, a growing population threatens birds and animals. Towns expand, roads are enlarged, grid lines span the countryside, and farmers cultivate every corner of their fields. Progress is necessary to mankind, regrettably it is often detrimental to the survival of wildlife. The natural habitat of many creatures shrinks annually, for animals, like man, are the victims of 'land hunger'. The answer to this problem can only be the building of vast nature reserves. In Britain, the National Parks are helping to preserve wildlife. The question is, inevitably, 'is enough being done soon enough?'

Population expansion and urban growth have arisen largely from industrial expansion. Too often, industrial expansion has meant that rivers have become polluted with poisonous chemicals and oils. Fish and birds are threatened alike. If science can be beneficial to man, by the same terms it can be made safe and beneficial to animals. To clean rivers and prevent air pollution will cost money . But, in the long run it will be cheap. For who can assess the value of any irreplaceable species of animal, bird or fish?

In recent years a new and sinister threat has arisen which could completely upset the delicate balance of nature. As Miss Rachel Carson has shown in her book 'Silent Spring', the effects of modern insecticides, used by progressive farmers, could damage numerous animals which feed on the insects. The poisons, sprayed on crops to kill insects can in turn kill animals and birds which feed on the insects. It is important to emphasise also that human beings eat these sprayed crops and the animals that feed on them. Drugs, designed to help human beings are tested thoroughly before they are marketed. Similarly, chemicals sprayed on the land to eliminate harmful pests must be tested also.

Man needs animals so that he himself can survive. He eats their flesh, he wears their hides and furs, he uses their products in endless ways. Many valuable chemicals are taken from animals. Again, birds, animals and fish enliven man's life. On a drab Decemday many people are cheered by the sight of robins and blue tits feeding outside their windows. Man cannot afford to hazard the existence of wildlife and controls must be established to safeguard the existence of animals. Finally, people must be made aware of the very real dangers in the world which now threatens all wildlife. For, without wildlife, man himself could become an extinct species.

CELTIC REVISION AIDS

Multiple Choice A Level Objective tests are now an important part of most A Level examinations. This series presents batteries of common questions and is also an excellent way of revising essential facts. Subjects covered in this series are: Pure Mathematics, Applied Mathematics, Chemistry, Physics, and Biology.

Test Yourself A series of pocket books designed for the revision of essential facts whenever the student has a free moment. Subjects covered in this series are: English, Language, French, German, Commerce, Economics, Mathematics, Modern Mathematics, Chemistry, Physics, Biology, and Human Biology.

Celtic Revision Aids can make the difference between passing or failing your examination.